Praise for *Permission to Speak Freely*

"*Permission to Speak Freely* is a rare leadership book that entertains and educates. The stories are memorable, the research is meaningful, and the takeaways are immediately actionable."
—**Adam Grant, Wharton professor and *New York Times* bestselling author of *Give and Take* and *Originals***

"We simply cannot figure out what is essential as leaders without people sharing what they are seeing, hearing, and experiencing. This takes powerful listening on the part of the leader. These truths—and how to make them a reality—are beautifully illustrated in this book."
—**Greg McKeown, *New York Times* bestselling author of *Essentialism***

"This book tackles the most important problem in organizations today—leaders do not know how to encourage their subordinates to speak up. *Permission to Speak Freely* not only identifies the problem with powerful stories but offers suggestions that are important to leaders at every level, especially those at the very tops of their organization."
—**Edgar H. Schein, Professor Emeritus, MIT Sloan School of Management, and author of *Humble Consulting* and *Humble Inquiry***

"Incredible writing. Edible lessons. I set out to read a chapter of *Permission to Speak Freely* and then couldn't put it down. Devour this book and learn from it."
—**Scott Snook, Senior Lecturer, Harvard Business School, and coauthor of *The Discover Your True North Fieldbook* and *The Handbook for Teaching Leadership***

"Crandall and Kincaid adroitly reveal how leaders inadvertently derail creativity and commitment, and deliver keen insights on how to avoid that trap. *Permission to Speak Freely* is a powerful reminder to leaders that they aren't necessarily the smartest people in the room."
—**Tom Kolditz, Founding Director, Ann and John Doerr Institute for New Leaders, Rice University; retired Brigadier General; and former Professor and Leadership Development Program Director, Yale School of Management**

"The tenets illustrated in *Permission to Speak Freely* are already shaping the way I operate my business, build my team, and consult on matters of organization change management. This book is a remarkable tool for diverse leaders worldwide."
—**Tyler Borders, cofounder and Principal, Dartlet**

Permission to Speak Freely

PERMISSION TO SPEAK FREELY

How the Best Leaders
Cultivate a Culture of Candor

DOUG CRANDALL and
MATT KINCAID, PhD

Berrett–Koehler Publishers, Inc.
a BK Business book

BERRETT-KOEHLER PUBLISHERS, INC.

1333 Broadway, Suite 1000, Oakland, CA 94612-1921

Tel: (510) 817-2277   Fax: (510) 817-2278   www.bkconnection.com

ORDERING INFORMATION

QUANTITY SALES. Special discounts are available on quantity purchases by corporations, associations, and others. For details, contact the "Special Sales Department" at the Berrett-Koehler address above.

INDIVIDUAL SALES. Berrett-Koehler publications are available through most bookstores. They can also be ordered directly from Berrett-Koehler:

Tel: (800) 929-2929; Fax: (802) 864-7626; www.bkconnection.com

ORDERS FOR COLLEGE TEXTBOOK/COURSE ADOPTION USE. Please contact Berrett-Koehler:

Tel: (800) 929-2929; Fax: (802) 864-7626.

ORDERS BY U.S. TRADE BOOKSTORES AND WHOLESALERS. Please contact Ingram Publisher Services, Tel: (800) 509-4887; Fax: (800) 838-1149; E-mail: customer.service@ingrampublisherservices.com; or visit www.ingrampublisherservices.com/Ordering for details about electronic ordering.

Berrett-Koehler and the BK logo are registered trademarks of Berrett-Koehler Publishers, Inc.

PRINTED IN THE UNITED STATES OF AMERICA

Berrett-Koehler books are printed on long-lasting acid-free paper. When it is available, we choose paper that has been manufactured by environmentally responsible processes. These may include using trees grown in sustainable forests, incorporating recycled paper, minimizing chlorine in bleaching, or recycling the energy produced at the paper mill.

LIBRARY OF CONGRESS CATALOGING-IN-PUBLICATION DATA

Names: Crandall, Doug, 1971– editor. | Kincaid, Matt, author.
Title: Permission to speak freely : how the best leaders cultivate a culture of candor / Doug Crandall and Matt Kincaid, PhD.
Description: First Edition. | Oakland : Berrett-Koehler Publishers, Inc., [2017]
Identifiers: LCCN 2016047233 | ISBN 9781626569225 (pbk.)
Subjects: LCSH: Leadership. | Communication in management.
Classification: LCC HD57.7 .C6963 2017 | DDC 658.4/092–dc23
LC record available at https://lccn.loc.gov/2016047233

FIRST EDITION

22 21 20 19 18 17   10 9 8 7 6 5 4 3 2 1

INTERIOR DESIGN: VJB/Scribe   EDIT: Elissa Rabellino
COVER DESIGN: Kirk DouPonce/DogEared Design   INDEX: Paula C. Durbin-Westby
PRODUCTION SERVICE: Linda Jupiter Productions PROOFREAD: Karen Hill Green

Contents

Contents

Foreword

One Saturday at the kitchen table, one of my early leadership mentors sat down with me, and what he said changed me for good. I'd been having difficulties understanding why I kept getting into relational conflicts that seemed to go from bad to worse, from calm to chaos, and from what I saw as logic to what I and others experienced as shame. He had watched me work, he'd seen me in my most beloved relationships, he had witnessed me on the continuum from my best to my worst. I knew he loved me and cared for me, and as I look back on that time, I remember how fortified I was with regard to others. I wanted to ward off all circumstances in which someone might speak of my faults. When it came to my own weaknesses, I was a fortress. I let no one in. Thankfully he had the courage to speak to me anyway.

He started with grace, describing how he valued our relationship, highlighting a few personal traits he saw as my strengths. He then spoke of his own weaknesses in a way that was both sincere and authentically transparent. Then he asked if I'd be willing to hear a few observations he'd made of the ways I handled conflict. I said yes, and as he proceeded I thought I'd hear him out fully and try to respond well. However, when he said, "When you get into conflict with others, you get extremely defensive," my face flushed and I felt a pit in my stomach. "No, I don't," I said.

Incredibly, despite the obvious hypocrisy of my response, I truly believed I was not defensive, and even more, I was willing to defend my truth to the grave! Unfortunately, sometimes what we call our own truths are actually false, and often they keep us from living a more whole, free, loving, and discerning life.

Do you remember a time in your life when a necessary, if uncomfortable, conversation changed you? If you do or if you don't, *Permission to Speak Freely*, the new book by cutting-edge leadership consultants Doug Crandall and Matt Kincaid, can help you generate the highest levels of personal and collective leadership: leadership that encourages the individual, the organization, the community, the family, and the nation to speak what needs to be spoken.

I grew up in Montana, land of one hundred mountain ranges. For a moment, picture walking along a high mountain plateau in the Beartooth Range along the southern border of Montana. Peaks rise over twelve thousand feet. But on the plateau below the tree line, the land contains multitudes: wildflowers like glacier lily and shooting star, animals like wolverine and what research biologists call *Ursus arctos horribilis*, the grizzly bear, humpbacked and powerful. Mountain swifts play the wind as if caught in an aerial symphony. At the summit, the land appears to kiss the sky. Here, all is visible for hundreds of miles, undulations of mountain ranges, valleys of great depth, rivers like silver ore running west to the Pacific and east to the Gulf. If you stay through the darkness, dawn is a new creation, spilling over the mountains, turning your face gold. In leadership, as in personal life, some understandings are this crystalline, this capable of helping us transcend ourselves, find humility, and live a more true existence. In *Permission to Speak Freely*, Matt and Doug give us a new vista and greater vision. They help us weather some of the most entangled and dangerous landscapes of humanity. By not only listening deeply, but encouraging those around us to speak freely, leaders can create organizations and communities that transcend the status quo and lead us into a future that is inspired, profound, and beautiful.

Give this book a transformative read. Let this book transform you.

See this book transform those around you with a new vision, far-reaching and filled with the kind of legitimate power that creates rather than degrades, and sees us through the darkness to the light of a new dawn.

Shann Ray Ferch, PhD
Professor, Leadership Studies
Gonzaga University
Author, *Forgiveness and Power in the Age of Atrocity: Servant Leadership as a Way of Life*, and *American Masculine: Stories*

HOW SPEAKING FREELY HELPED BRING A CHAMPIONSHIP TO SEATTLE

Multipliers . . . don't focus on what they know but on how to know what others know. . . . They are interested in every relevant insight people can offer.[1]

—*LIZ WISEMAN*, MULTIPLIERS

During the 2013 National Football League season, the Seattle Seahawks paid Steven Hauschka $715,000 to kick a football through the uprights when the team needed three points. Hauschka was a worthy employee, successfully converting thirty-three of his thirty-five three-point attempts during the sixteen-game campaign. His success rate in 2013 placed him second in NFL field goal accuracy.

Hauschka had never even kicked a football in a competitive setting until fall 2004—his third semester at Vermont's Middlebury College. He was cut from the varsity soccer team as a freshman, so at the outset of sophomore year, his roommate urged him to try out for the football team. Middlebury desperately needed a kicker. Hauschka made the team and went on to set numerous records over three years. After finishing up at Middlebury with a degree in neuroscience, he went on to a year of graduate school at North Carolina State, where he also served as the Wolfpack's field goal kicker.

Hauschka's successful season kicking for a Division I college football program caught the attention of the Minnesota Vikings, who signed him to their preseason squad as an undrafted free agent. He didn't make the team, however, and spent the next three years wandering the NFL.

Hauschka's success with the Seahawks continued into 2014 as the team made a run toward the Super Bowl. Early in the fourth quarter of the NFC Championship game versus the San Francisco 49ers, Pete Carroll called on his kicker for a fourth-down, fifty-three-yard field goal that would bring the Seahawks within one point of the lead. The importance of the moment was not lost on any Seattle fan. It had been thirty-five years since any major, professional sports team had won a championship for the city. The 2013–14 Seahawks had a chance to not only win the Super Bowl but end the long suffering for the sports fans of an entire region.

Steven Hauschka—the wanderer who had finally found some job security with the Seahawks—was about to trot on the field for one of the most important kicks of his career. But as he passed by Pete Carroll, Hauschka noticed the wind marker at the top of the north upright whipping swiftly in the southerly direction. He gave it a quick thought and decided that the field goal attempt was not the right decision. This guy, whom Seahawks owner Paul Allen was paying three quarters of a million dollars per year to kick a football, didn't want to do it. So what did Hauschka do? He buckled down, thought positive, and made the kick . . .

No. That is *not* what Steven Hauschka did in that moment. Instead, he turned to his coach and stated plainly, "We shouldn't kick this." He then ran onto the turf and stared at the spot where the football was to be placed. A few second later, Carroll called time-out. From the stands, or the comfort of a living room, it was a curious scene. The kicker had taken his spot on the field and waited for the snap and placement of the ball, only to be called back to the sideline.

Carroll had listened. The Seahawks would not have Hauschka attempt a field goal, in this moment. A series of events that appeared puzzling to fans would make perfect sense after the game: an employee had provided input into a decision and his leader had adjusted course. Hauschka's journey from Middlebury College to undrafted free agent to wanderer to somewhat-stable Seahawks employee undoubtedly hovered over his relationship with his boss. He likely felt fortunate to have any job at all. His status as lowly kicker also weighed in. While important at critical times, field goal specialists are usually low-status members of any NFL team. Pete Carroll's expected response to Steven Hauschka's input?

"I made the call. Just do your job, kicker."

In fact, direct reports of Carroll standing in earshot of the head coach could hardly believe that Hauschka would even open his mouth. Carroll, on the other hand, welcomed the candor, especially from the guy who knew this part of the "business" better than anyone else on the team: "I love the honesty. Most guys say, 'I can make it and go out there and plunk it down at the goal line.' I thought it was a great moment for us, and it was a great decision."[2]

Doug's wife recommended that we not begin this book with the Hauschka example. Thousands of San Francisco 49er fans would be bound to stop reading, she warned. Many college football enthusiasts hate Pete Carroll and think he cheated as a college coach at USC. People in New York and Boston remember his failed tenures with the Jets and

Patriots. But the fact remains: In 2014, Pete Carroll was the overwhelming winner when ESPN asked 230 NFL players, "Which head coach would you most like to play for?" Carroll garnered 23 percent of the votes, far outpacing Mike Tomlin of the Pittsburgh Steelers, who received 14 percent. No other head coach reached double digits.

Reflecting on the survey results, Carroll observed, "We're open around here. We're honest enough and straightforward enough that we can talk right to our guys about any issue in front of the rest of the team."[3] Honest enough and open enough that when Steven Hauschka didn't think he would convert a critical field goal attempt, he was willing to say so.

> "I didn't think it was the right decision,
> and I let Coach Carroll know that."

Carroll called a time-out; the offense went back on the field. Many thousands of fans turned to each other and wondered what was going on. Moments later, Russell Wilson threw a thirty-six-yard touchdown strike that gave the Seahawks the lead in the fourth quarter—a lead they would not relinquish. Seahawks fans went wild. 49ers fans shook their heads. Steven Hauschka, lowly kicker—at one of the most critical moments of his career—felt empowered to question his coach's decision. In fact, he didn't just question the decision; he told Pete Carroll that it was not a good one. Equally important, Carroll listened.

The Seattle Seahawks won Super Bowl XLVIII in resounding fashion, bringing the Emerald City its first title in thirty-five years. Just a few days later, over a half a million people lined the streets from KeyArena to CenturyLink Field. Riding on a Washington National Guard cargo truck, waving to fans stacked ten deep on the sidewalks, Hauschka celebrated with his teammates. He had made nine kicks in nine attempts in the playoffs. But the most important one of the season was probably the one he didn't take. The Seattle Seahawks were Super Bowl champions—in part—because of Hauschka's willingness to speak freely to his head coach. And Pete Carroll was the most popular coach among NFL players—in part—because of the culture he had forged: one of openness, where he valued the input of every member of the team—even the journeyman kicker.

This book is for leaders of any kind. If you are a leader, people will hesitate to tell you what they're truly thinking. They will hesitate to question—especially your ideas. They will hesitate to share their own ideas. They will hesitate to ask for help. They will hesitate to point out mistakes and admit mistakes. They will hesitate to call out lapses of integrity. And in many organizations, the hesitation will become suffocation and no one will say anything at all. Yet study after study finds that candid communication enhances innovation, ownership, engagement, and overall performance. As Jim Collins observes in his best-selling classic *Good to Great*, "Leadership is about creating a climate where the truth is heard and the brutal facts are confronted."[4]

Therein lies the opportunity of this book and a new way of thinking about the valuable insights of those we serve as leaders. Within a Speak Freely culture, ideas thrive, sacred cows die, and decisions improve. Anesthetic soft talk is the archenemy of true leadership. Typically we envision ourselves—the leaders—as the ones who must talk straight. We're not arguing against that. But flip that notion upside down and focus on those you lead speaking candidly to you. Everything you hear will make your organization and you better. It may sting at first, but the advantages of open communication previously mentioned—greater innovation, ownership, engagement, and overall performance—are beyond debate.

Counterexamples litter the leadership landscape in iconic form: Watergate, the space shuttle disasters, Quaker's $1.4 billion loss on the purchase of Snapple, Jerry Sandusky's crimes at Penn State, a problematic launch of the Obamacare website: in each of these examples, someone failed to speak up, failed to listen, or both. Silence, or at best timid suggestion, is the norm in most organizations. So how do leaders create an environment where people will speak freely to each other without fear of reprisal, embarrassment, condemnation, or even rolling eyeballs? How do leaders create a place where team members speak openly, anytime, and all the time?

This book seeks to provide answers to these questions and offers tools for leaders who want to build flourishing organizations where there is ample room and encouragement for every voice. Part 1 outlines the three key things that leaders hear from their employees, their players, or anyone they're leading in a culture where everyone has permission to speak freely. Part 2 provides a research-backed case illustrating the barriers to open communication and gives cautionary warnings for conversation killers that leaders must be on the lookout for. The final section, part 3, offers practical tools for leaders to utilize in cultivating a culture of candor and concludes with a depiction of a tremendous organization reaping its benefits.

PART ONE

WHAT LEADERS NEED TO HEAR

QUESTIONS AND UNCERTAINTIES

There are naïve questions, tedious questions, ill-phrased questions. . . . But every question is a cry to understand the world. There is no such thing as a dumb question.

—*CARL SAGAN*, THE DEMON-HAUNTED WORLD

We had a student, Paul, who was investigating a given career path and needed some help. One of us reached out to Micah—a friend in that field. Micah suggested that our student talk to a woman named Lisa, and we passed this info on to Paul via email. Shortly after, a text exchange followed:

PAUL: So email both of those two people?

US: Email Lisa and copy Micah.

PAUL: Like copy his email? Sorry I probably sound dumb.

US: When you send an email you can "copy" someone by putting them in the "cc" address. This means you're sending it to Lisa but letting Micah know what's going on.

PAUL: Oh, okay.

US: You don't sound dumb.

When people expose themselves as unknowing, they immediately feel vulnerable. If they speak up and ask a question, they will search for the right way to ask—a way that doesn't sound "dumb." The leader's response to their questions will have a significant impact on whether or not they ask again. And a culture of candor or a culture of silence will have been reinforced. It happens that quickly.

As leader developers, we've seen the boundless benefits of people speaking freely—and embracing a culture of candor. It happens when you release people from the burden of saying things the *right* way. As leaders, we should be cultivating questions, doubts, uncertainties, and other variations of not knowing. When people have permission to speak freely, they will put forth their perspectives, ask when they don't understand, and seek guidance when they need help. So ask yourself:

> Do I welcome a spirit of speaking freely?
> Do I *really* welcome it?

Let those questions echo within you for a few seconds. Do you want to hear the questions and uncertainties that the people you lead wish they could say, want to say, aren't sure they should say, feel vulnerable saying, and hold back from bringing up simply because they can't find the *right* words? We believe all leaders need to hear the unfiltered thoughts and ideas from their people. What we're proposing in this book is that you hear everything. Literally everything. You may be thinking, "I don't want to hear everything. I don't have time." We hope this book will change your mind. The benefits of candid communication are immense and often life altering. Let's look at a simple example of speaking up in confusion.

One Sunday afternoon, ten-year-old Timmy appeared to halfheartedly play through the first two quarters of a youth basketball game. He was jogging up and down the court, and his defense lacked intensity. Few things will accelerate the pulse of a basketball coach (or an overbearing father) more quickly than lackadaisical defense. In this case, the spectating father turned to his daughter midway through the first half and grumbled, "What's the deal with your brother? Look at him. He has his back to the ball and he's completely lost his man." If you're unfamiliar with basketball, one of the most important defensive principles is that every player should have his or her "head on a swivel" and be able to see both the person he or she is guarding and the basketball, at the same time, at all times. Timmy wasn't doing this.

On the way home from the game, Timmy's father broached the subject of proper defensive technique. His sermon lasted for about three minutes, during which he told Timmy, "Don't turn your back to the ball," six or seven times. "It's about giving it 100 percent. You're capable of playing great defense. Stuff like turning your back to the ball is all about effort," huffed his father. The conversation stifled, and Timmy slowly grew more and more agitated. Finally his anger and frustration boiled over and he screamed out with tears in his eyes, "I don't even know what you mean! I don't know what you're talking about when you say 'Don't turn your back on the ball'!"

There's so much power in speaking freely, whether it's a ten-year-old after a basketball game, a school janitor, a new manager, a rookie baseball player, a private first class in the military, or a commercial airline copilot. If Timmy doesn't speak up in that moment, his dad assumes that he got the message. And because he had no idea what his father meant, his silence means that everything his dad said has been lost on him. Nobody benefits. The next time his father sees Timmy turn his back to the ball, he will assume that Timmy blew him off. And because he told Timmy six or seven times during the car ride, he concludes that his son lacks respect or just doesn't care. The situation spirals downward at an accelerated rate. Three months later, he fires him. And while a dad can't fire a son from the family, you get the point—this isn't just a youth basketball story. It's a story about leadership and communication. Leaders often mistake a lack of clarity for defiance. Timmy was confused, but his willingness to speak up saved the moment.

The reason that a *permission to speak freely* leadership orientation is so critical is because it's so different. We all recognize organizational silence as a problem. It's not a novel idea. But collectively, we've attempted to solve this problem in the wrong way. There are a handful of best-selling books aimed at teaching followers how to articulate their thoughts effectively, or how to speak courageously, or how to speak persuasively in an upward direction. Millions of dollars are spent on communication training each year. Timmy had neither read any of these books nor been trained in how to see things from his dad's perspective. He just boiled over and spoke freely: "I don't even know what you mean!" And truthfully, his dad was lucky that he spoke up at all. As leaders, we can't rely on luck. It's our job to initiate these conversations and build a culture where speaking freely is the norm and where people never ask for permission to speak freely—they simply know it's been granted.

Dan Lovallo, from the University of Sydney, and Olivier Sibony, from McKinsey and Company—who've done extensive research on the role of inclusion and voice in decision-making—observe, "The culture of many organizations suppresses uncertainty and rewards behavior that ignores it . . . seldom do we see confidence as a warning sign—a hint that overconfidence, overoptimism, and other action-oriented biases may be at work."[1] Whether because of culture, incentive structures, insecurity, or inexperience, Jeff Gaines found himself in a situation where he needed help but forged on with "confidence."

Gaines started out as an hourly associate at one of the world's largest retailers. He earned a college degree on the side and then rapidly worked his way through the company's merchandising ranks to become one of its youngest directors. Identified as "top talent," Gaines earned a nomination to the company's high-potential leadership program and a promotion to senior director. The original pilot of the leadership development course included an exercise designed to place front-line leaders and headquarters executives in the shoes of their own constituents: the Core Customer Challenge. Because of the emotional impact of the event, it has maintained its place in the curriculum through multiple years of revisions.

Per the challenge, Gaines and his cohort of eight colleagues set out one afternoon to purchase a week's worth of groceries for a family of four living just above the poverty line. The budget was just under $70 (yes, for the entire week). Thirty minutes later, with milk, breakfast cereal, and a loaf of bread loaded in their shopping cart, Gaines and his group stood in front of the canned vegetables looking for the least expensive offering of green beans. Situated prominently on the middle shelf, the company's private label was the best bargain at $0.68. A woman on Gaines's team grabbed two cans and tossed them in the cart. Gaines, though, stopped the group before they could move on. "Just a second," he murmured, "there are some cheaper ones down there."

"Down there" was on the bottom right, out of the sight line of the average-sized human. Jeff spotted the Three Charms–brand beans—priced at $0.52 per can—because he had put them on the bottom shelf two years earlier while fighting his way up the merchandising ranks as a canned-vegetable buyer.* When Three Charms came to Jeff with their original pitch, he was hesitant to make the beans part of his assortment. Although doing so would be consistent with company strategy (offering the lowest price point of any retailer), the company's mission (helping people save money), and Gaines's own values, it conflicted with his incentive structure. His target for the year was a 4 percent revenue increase in his category. His performance review and bonus depended on it. At the point when he met Three Charms, he was trending just above 3 percent growth and working hard to improve. Placing Three Charms beans on the shelf—in a prominent position—would reduce sales of more expensive beans, slowing Gaines's revenue growth. In the end, it wasn't his conscience or his concern for the customer that put those beans on the shelf. From a strategy standpoint, he simply knew that he needed to introduce the lowest-priced option. So if he had to do it, he'd protect his

---

* We've omitted the company's name and changed the brand to "Three Charms" on the advice of counsel (their counsel).

revenues in the process. Hiding Three Charms in the bottom right solved the problem. Gaines never shared his concerns with his boss. When the two of them went through his display plan, he justified the placement of Three Charms beans through a number of logical arguments. None of them included what he was really thinking: *I'm trying to hide them.*

Most will empathize with the push and pull of Gaines's competing interests: customers, strategy, and his own job performance. In his mid-twenties, trying to launch a long-term career with the company, he had three reasonable options:

1. reject Three Charms;

2. put the new brand of beans on the shelf; or

3. make Three Charms available, but in a place where customers probably wouldn't see the beans.

In the world in which many of us reside—the one where people measure their words, hide their thoughts, and speak only when they know it's safe—Gaines settled on the hide-and-seek-the-beans option. Speak Freely leadership creates a fourth possibility: Jeff Gaines shares his uncertainty with his leader and asks for help:

> You know, boss, if I put the Three Charms beans right in the middle, it will cannibalize my other sales. My revenues will drop below target, and I won't get my bonus. I'll look like I'm failing. But I can't *not* offer them. They are the lowest price on the market. I want to do what's right for the customer and company, but

I'm not going to make 4 percent if I do that. I don't know what to do. I need your help.

We've queried thousands of leaders regarding scenarios similar to Three Charms beans. Literally *no one* has ever stood up in one of our classrooms and suggested that they wouldn't want to hear Gaines's vulnerable admission and request for guidance. The benefits of this type of candor are immediate and self-evident: instead of his placing the product below the normal customer's sight line, he uncovers a different solution with his boss. The company benefits. The customer benefits. Gaines does the right thing. Trust ensues, and he opens up a little more confidently the next time he faces a dilemma. And to be clear, this story is not about retail strategy, Jeff Gaines, beans, or even values and mission. It's simpler than that. It's about open communication in an upward direction. If you're Gaines's leader, you should want to know what he's *actually* thinking. You should want him to come to you for help if he needs it. You should want him to speak freely.

Permission to speak freely means, first and foremost, that the people you lead trust you enough to tell you they need help, to ask when they don't understand, and to be bold with their lack of clarity. When these thoughts start to pour out, others will follow.

GREAT IDEAS AND TERRIBLE ONES

You can't just give someone a creativity injection. You have to create an environment for curiosity and a way to encourage people and get the best out of them.

—SIR KEN ROBINSON, BLOOMBERG INTERVIEW, FEBRUARY 22, 2006

When organizations empower every person—at every level—to share ideas, innovation thrives, engagement scores go up, and feelings of ownership increase. This short chapter could almost qualify for the "tell me something I don't know" category, so we'll tell you something you probably don't know.

It turns out we all have a blind spot when it comes to hearing others' ideas—a big one worthy of discussion: people tend to harbor a hidden bias against creativity. Almost no one will say it out loud, but research suggests that it's close to universally true. We prefer known solutions, especially in times of uncertainty. Ironically, it's at times of uncertainty that creative solutions are often most needed. Leaders will opt for slightly new ideas, but don't go shouting "Earth revolves around the sun" on us or you're bound to get shot down. "American culture worships creativity," stated an article in *The Atlantic* in October 2014, "but mostly in the abstract." In order to gain idea acceptance, the writer recommended that people "frame new ideas as old ideas— to make your creativity seem, well, not so creative."[1] Not bad advice for those suffering under the thumb of tone-deaf leadership, but not the advice of this book. As leaders, we must stop holding our people prisoner to the idea that they must present all thoughts and ideas the *right* way—that is, the way that keeps us feeling comfortable.

Did you know that former Microsoft CEO Steve Ballmer predicted the iPhone would never gain traction? Decca Records, in a first-ever audition, famously told the Beatles that groups like theirs had gone out of style. In 1927, Harry Warner of Warner Bros. Pictures asked, "Who the hell wants to hear actors talk?" Executives at ABC shook their heads in amusement when Lloyd Braun first proposed the television series *Lost*. You might have heard that E. L. James self-published *Fifty Shades of Grey* after widespread rejection, but did you know that Mark Twain self-published *The Adventures of Huckleberry Finn*? And yes, every studio in Hollywood rejected *Raiders of the Lost Ark*. Point being: As leaders, we need as much help as we can get. If we don't capitalize on those around us, our own abilities and ideas become the maximum capacity of the teams we ostensibly lead. We need creative ideas, slaps in the face, and warnings of impending doom. We need to listen, and we need to listen well, so that our people break through the aforementioned obstacles, believe in their ideas, and start speaking up.

In his book *Drive*, Daniel Pink teaches that mental parameters such as, in this instance, trying to find the right way to say something to your boss, significantly hinder creative thinking.[2] Communication is hard enough when people say what they mean. So as long as the people you lead are focused on cracking your language code—or trying to say things the way they imagine you want to hear them—they're no doubt giving you a lot of crappy suggestions. And this forces you to tighten the reins even more, right? Of course, you have to micromanage because your people can't think for themselves—and it's true, they can't. Not under the scrutiny and fear of having to articulate their own ideas into your personal safe language for them to even be heard.

Instead of responding based on your own discomfort and uncertainty when you hear a new idea, force yourself to stop and at least listen. Just listen. Take a deep breath, bite your tongue, and hear what your people have to say. Listen, not while preparing a rebuttal in your head, but so you hear. In executive coaching terms, it's called *active listening*. You'll hear amazing "new" ideas. And your people will respect you more and be eager to share all the awesome things they've kept locked in their mental vault for years because they've been shut down by someone, somewhere, and been afraid to speak candidly.

And you must listen to the good and the "bad."

Sometime prior to 1993, Pacific Power and Light gathered a team to address the debilitating effects of inclement weather.[3] Freezing temperatures often conspired with the moisture of the Pacific Northwest to leave power lines cocooned in ice. When harsh conditions persisted over a matter of days, the weight of the ice would cause the lines to stress and ultimately snap. The hazard forced Pacific Power to send its workers into the field to climb the poles and, with long hooks, shake the lines. It was a nasty and dangerous job.

Several attempts to solve the case of the icy power lines proved fruitless. The company eventually brought some of the front-line technicians into the brainstorming mix.

Intimidated, many of these workers sat quietly and listened to the ideas of others. But during a break, a Pacific Power executive overheard one of the company's operators complain to his buddy: "I hate that crazy job. Last week, I fell off the slippery pole. When I landed, I was peering into the eyes of an enormous black bear. He did not seem to like me invading his territory."

"We should just train the bears to climb the poles and shake the ice off," his friend responded. "Black bears are best."*

In a meeting room full of executives they did not trust, these two hands-on professionals remained silent. But during a bathroom break, they became the key to steamrolling an entire morning of barricaded creativity. The Pacific Power manager who overheard the idea asked friend number two to share what he had said during the break. He figured it to be mostly nonsensical but thought it might lubricate some further discussion. On cue, the rest of the group laughed when the gentleman suggested his bear-training technique. Full-blown judgment and disapproval immediately took hold.

Either feeling uncomfortable with the laughter directed at his colleague or genuinely attempting to forward the dialogue, a different line worker raised his hand. "It might be tough to train the bears to do that, but what if we put honey pots at the top of the electric poles? The bears would climb the poles to get the honey and knock the ice off the wires."

---

*The black bear quote is entirely for fans of The Office. You can't spend months writing a book and not have a little fun.

The discussion gained a slight tone of sincerity and a manager asked: "How is that better than what we have now? We'd have to get the honey pots on top of the poles."

A crusty senior line worker chimed in with a voice of indignation. "Our execs are always flying around in their fancy helicopters. Why don't we just use the choppers for some good and fly around placing honey pots on poles?" Smatters of laughter bounced around the room until a secretary spoke up. "I was a nurse's aide in Vietnam. Casualties were always flying into our field hospital on helicopters. The downwash from the helicopter blades threw everything around. The dust and the debris would almost blind us. Why don't we just fly the helicopters over the power lines and let the rotors knock the ice off?" From bears to honey pots to helicopters, a secretary at Pacific Power and Light—a woman willing to speak freely in that moment—crafted a solution that the company used for decades.

Questions and uncertainties come first. It takes patience and self-awareness to hear the seemingly naive, ignorant, or repetitive, and reject the urge to judge them as "dumb." Ideas will come next—the good and the bad. And once ideas have been shared and validated, feedback and concerns will surface.

FEEDBACK AND CONCERNS

There are only two mistakes one can make
along the road to truth:
not going all the way, and not starting.

—BUDDHA

What's the most difficult "truth" you've ever had to deliver to someone? Think about it for a moment before you read on. Whom did you have to talk to, and what did you need to tell him or her? Did you actually do it? How did you feel, physically and emotionally, before the conversation? How did you feel afterward?

Our guess is, whatever this conversation entailed, you tried to use the right words in the right way; maybe you even practiced beforehand or sought advice from a friend. But in the end, there may just not have been a "right" way to say it. Yet you said it anyway because it needed to be said. You likely hoped the recipient would trust your intent, hear the message, and simply move forward with the new (or added) perspective. A relationship may have been damaged, or maybe your message landed upon grateful ears. You might have felt relieved, appreciated, or horrified. You may have received a "Thank you for your courage," or maybe you were fired.

Here's the point, and it's the primary point we hope to impress upon you in the context of this book: when your people have permission to speak freely, they say these things to you . . . and they say them without reservation, without worrying about the right words, and without anxiety or apprehension. They have. Permission. To Speak. Freely.

This is radical. It's rare. It's invaluable. And it unleashes a culture of trust and empowerment present in only the best of organizations. It's also entirely achievable when leaders are willing to set aside ego, and battle (yes battle) through the demons that will arise when those you lead share their candid feedback and concerns. Chapter 1 explained that opening up to questions and uncertainties requires patience and emotional intelligence. Chapter 2 discussed the fact that listening to others' ideas requires setting aside our hidden bias against creativity and tendency to defer to the status quo. But opening up to feedback and concerns is another level . . . this requires the heart of a servant leader and the setting aside of ego and our own insecurities.

We've collectively spent more than two decades helping develop leaders in university settings and within organizations all across the United States. In all of our programs, we attempt to create the type of environment we've described in the opening chapters. We want to hear every question or uncertainty, every idea, and any feedback or concern. A few years ago, a student approached Doug to discuss a grade. After several minutes of some back and forth about a particular test, Jocelyn looked down at her feet briefly and then bellowed:

"Why don't you love your daughter?"

We could construct three different drafts of better ways for Jocelyn to have raised this concern. It was, in fact, a statement framed as a question (as feedback and concerns often are). In one sense, it was a triumph of teaching—Jocelyn had spoken freely. On the other hand, it was a tremendous challenge to Doug's character. Jocelyn had skipped "Do you love your daughter?" and gone straight to the conclusion. But we deeply believe in every word we've written in this book. *Releasing the people you lead from the burden of saying things the right way* means getting past Jocelyn's articulation.

Truth be told, Doug's first unspoken thought upon hearing this student's question was: "Hmmm . . . well, Jocelyn, don't bring your issues with your own dad to this office." But, stepping back, this was a speak-freely moment of immense proportions. Doug holds love of family as one of his core values. Jocelyn had questioned that. In this moment, we also experienced one of the truths behind the challenge of letting others speak freely: the greater the power gap, the easier this task. When a student questions your parental integrity, you demonstrate some patience and grace and consider the issue at hand. When your neighbor questions it, your ego flares and your defenses go up. But your ego has nothing to do with the truth and accuracy of the message at hand. It serves us as leaders to listen either way and seek greater understanding.

"Why would you ask that, Jocelyn?"

"Well, you tell stories about your sons all the time, but you never talk about your daughter."

Here's the skillfully prepared version of what Jocelyn was trying to say: "You tell lots of stories about your sons, which I always enjoy. But I don't recall you telling any stories about your daughter. Although it might not be your intent, this gives me the impression that you aren't as interested in her activities, or possibly women in general. Honestly, it makes me wonder whether you care about me as much as some of the men in the class."

Jocelyn served up an important message that day. She was right—Doug did not tell as many stories about his daughter, which gave the impression that he didn't care about her as much as he did his sons. It's a message we never would have heard if we had placed the burden of gifted communication upon Jocelyn, if we had shut down her concern, or if we didn't listen to her feedback and act upon it (by telling some daughter stories in the future).

Somewhere, among the people you lead, are bits and chunks and boulders of things they need to say—or may someday need to say. Matters of conscience, integrity, decision-making, or behavior, or just stories about sons and daughters. Given permission to speak freely, our organizations are protected from the ills of groupthink, collusion, blind spots, intimidation, confirmation bias, integrity lapses, and other maladies.

The two researchers we introduced in chapter 1, Dan Lovallo and Olivier Sibony, investigated 1,048 business decisions over five years. During the course of their research, they made countless inquiries into decision-making processes, asking the following questions (among others):

Did discussion include perspectives that contradicted the senior executive's point of view?

Did [the executives] elicit participation from a range of people who had a different view of the decision?

The pair also exhaustively studied the level and quality of analytical rigor contributing to each of the thousand-plus decisions. The Lovallo-Sibony research zeroed in on a profound conclusion that all leaders should consider when cultivating an environment where feedback and concerns flow freely:

Process mattered more than analysis by a factor of six.

When launching products, acquiring businesses, altering corporate structure, or deciding whom to hire and fire, analysis matters; but the benefits of debate, discussion, skepticism, and scrutiny matter six times more. Absent an authentic and vibrant process, "good analysis in the hands of good managers won't naturally yield good decisions." Jim Collins echoes this idea in his book *Good to Great*: "You absolutely cannot make a series of good decisions without confronting the brutal facts."[1]

As leaders, we must create a climate where the people we lead share with us their concerns and feedback—brutal and all—without hesitation. We *need* the lowly kickers of the world, at the most critical moments in an NFL season, with all its associated pressures and urgencies mounting, to look us in the eye and warn: "We shouldn't kick this." And as much as it may sting, when someone we lead has a concern but no perfect way to share it with us, we *need* him or her to confront us with the raw, unfiltered question, "Why don't you love your daughter?"

But to do so, we must first understand what gets in the way . . .

And Mackenzie, I love you with all my heart :)

PART TWO

THE PROBLEM

LEADERS IMPEDE COMMUNICATION

We realize the importance of our voices only when we are silenced.

—*MALALA YOUSAFZAI,* I AM MALALA

Gary Stasser of Miami (Ohio) University conducted a seminal study on group communication based on a murder mystery scenario, titled *The Case of the Fallen Businessman*. Stasser discovered that open communication is difficult in small groups. People tend to share common knowledge but are afraid of looking foolish by voicing things only they know. Group members question themselves: *If it's relevant, why has no one else brought this up?* We've created a condensed version of this case study to illustrate Stasser's discoveries and to set the stage for further exploration into communication challenges.

The sun had just peeked over an eastern hill on a fall morning in 1992 when Eddie Sullivan pulled his rusty-red Ford truck into the carport on Bob Guion's homestead. Sullivan served as Guion's handyman, and he liked to start his work early to avoid the heat. This particular day, he was scheduled to tear down an eighty-year-old barn.

A few hours into the demolition, Sullivan realized that he'd left his crowbar back at his truck. It was several hundred yards away, but he needed the tool. When he reached the vehicle—around 10 a.m.—the crowbar was gone. "I looked all around," recalled Sullivan, "and that's when I saw Mr. Guion lying in the grass through the breezeway." Sullivan glanced briefly at Bob Guion's bloody, contorted body and dashed up the weathered staircase in a panic to pound on the door. "Call an ambulance!" he yelled to Marion Guion, Bob's wife. The police reports suggested that Bob Guion— owner of a local Lincoln dealership—had been assaulted and struck on the left brow as he exited the house for his regular 7 a.m. golf game. Lieutenant Mark Moody, lead investigator, named three primary suspects: Mickey Malone, a parts supplier to Guion's car dealership; Billy Prentice, the yardman; and Eddie Sullivan, the handyman who first discovered Guion's body.

Moody's focus quickly turned to Malone, whose motive seemed strongest (albeit still questionable). Just a week before the murder, Malone had received a handwritten note from Guion voicing displeasure with their business interactions. The note read:

> I am very upset about the substandard parts I have been receiving from you...I will have to notify my customers and other dealers about the quality of MM auto parts.

Harsh words, but would the 1992 equivalent of a one-star Yelp rating really be an impetus for murder? Malone admitted he'd been headed to Guion's property that Saturday, ready to confront Guion about the letter. But he'd thought better of it, U-turned on Crestview Highway, and stopped to get some coffee before arriving at the golf course at 7 a.m.

The second suspect, Billy Prentice, had a gambling problem and often approached "Mr. Bob" to borrow money. He'd done so as recently as the afternoon before Guion's death. But this dependence on his boss seemed almost a disincentive to kill him. Absent motive, Prentice proved a dubious suspect—until Moody discovered that he had lied in his initial statement, and his fingerprints had been found on the missing crowbar. Confronted with these facts, Prentice reversed course and admitted to having been on the property, but said he'd discovered Guion dead at the base of the stairs and fled in fear. He had no idea how his fingerprints had gotten on the crowbar or how it had ended up in the bushes.

The final suspect, Eddie Sullivan, pointed a limp finger at Prentice, suggesting that he'd heard a "car with a loud muffler" speeding away at about 7 a.m. The noise was tough to make out from the barn, but he was pretty sure that it was Prentice. The sound of an accelerating car didn't amount to a murder conviction, but the lying, fingerprints, and gambling problem all constituted a growing pile of circumstantial evidence. Moody just couldn't imagine what Billy Prentice's motive would have been.

Sullivan might have had a motive. His daughter had worked as the bookkeeper at Guion's dealership until quitting a few weeks before the murder. He claimed that he didn't know why his daughter left, but testimony from employees at the dealership revealed that her resignation had followed a heated argument with Guion. Body language and subtleties in one of the witness interviews even hinted at a possible affair.

But that was it: three suspects, a bunch of circumstantial evidence, and nowhere else to turn. DNA evidence, first used to convict Florida rapist Tommie Lee Andrews in 1987, was still considered a novelty in most venues as late as the mid-1990s. Whoever killed Bob Guion—whether Mickey Malone, Billy Prentice, Eddie Sullivan, or someone else—was going to get away with it.

So what if we asked you to take your best guess? Based on the information we presented summarizing the murder of Bob Guion, whom would you choose: Malone, Prentice, or Sullivan? With what amount of certainty would you cast your vote? It wouldn't be "beyond a reasonable doubt," but how about "more likely than not"?

Let's take it a step further. You've been designated the leader of a small group, charged with poring over the maps, notes, and interviews collected at the time of the killing. Justice—and a widow's peace of mind—depend on your team's ability to unlock the mystery of this cold case. And although you don't know it, among the stack of notes and interviews are pieces of information that will help you identify, unequivocally, the person who struck Bob Guion with Sullivan's crowbar and sent him down the rickety staircase to his death.

One member of your group holds the transcript of an interview with Millie Smith from Ray's Café. Her statement clears Mickey Malone. She corroborates that he was drinking coffee at Ray's from 6:30 a.m. to 6:45 a.m. Another team member knows that Prentice does, in fact, recall touching the crowbar, but only to move it so that he could get the lawnmower out of the covered parking area. This person also holds a statement from Dave Daniels, owner of a Quick Stop just down the street from Guion's house. Daniels found Guion's wallet around 7 a.m. Someone had thrown it toward the garbage bin behind the store and sped away. Whoever ditched the wallet was in a car that "ran real quiet."

Last are statements from Marion Guion. Not everyone you lead in this effort to solve the murder knows that Mrs. Guion had looked out her window at 6:40 a.m. All she saw in the covered parking area was Bob's pickup. She also informed police that Sullivan has a hearing aid but never wears it when he works.

Mickey Malone didn't kill Bob Guion. He has an alibi. Billy Prentice had no motive, he was completely forthright (after he wasn't), and it wasn't his loud truck that had dumped the wallet next to Dave Daniels's garbage bin. So the good news for your team? You can pinpoint Eddie Sullivan as the killer. He lied when he claimed to have heard Billy's truck. He couldn't have identified the low-quality muffler from several hundred yards away without the benefit of his hearing aid. He had motive and opportunity, and when Marion looked out the window at 6:40 a.m., Sullivan's truck was gone.*

In conducting this case study research, Stasser discovered that open communication is difficult in small groups. But

---

*Thanks to Gary Stasser of Miami University (Ohio) for sharing his murder mystery scenario. Stasser first used the scenario in 1992 as part of a series of studies on group communication.

this bad news gets even worse when formal leaders enter the fray. Research demonstrates that leaders often get in the way of solving problems, as power wreaks all kinds of havoc:

It elevates a leader's tendency to objectify others (leaders see others as a means to their ends).

It renders a leader tone-deaf to others' perspectives.

It leaves a leader more prone to stereotype.

It depletes a leader's willingness to listen.

Power is so powerful, in fact, that when Leigh Plunkett Tost, Francesca Gino, and Richard Larrick put power-primed leaders in charge of a team tasked to solve the Bob Guion murder, the leaders failed miserably.[1] Groups with formal leaders who had been primed to feel powerful tagged Eddie Sullivan as the culprit only 25 percent of the time. On the other hand, where there was no leader at all, groups solved the mystery 59 percent of the time. Astounding difference. Put more plainly: when placed in charge, leaders puff out their chests, run their mouths, and get in the way.

"Powerful" leader: 25 percent success

No leader at all: 59 percent success

In the murder mystery experiment, random participants wore name tags designating them as leaders. That's it. A name tag and an induced feeling of power (via pre-experiment reflection) resulted in communication-stifling dominance. Tost, Gino, and Larrick discovered that leaders who feel powerful talk too much. They dominate group discussions, shutting others down and devaluing them personally.

A few years ago, a participant in one of our programs made a courageous admission to the group: "I constantly have discussions with my team where I'm just trying to lead them to my idea and get their buy-in." Hesitantly, but almost therapeutically, she continued, "I've been promoted all along because people said I had great ideas. I guess it's hard to stop being the one with the ideas and instead be someone who gets others to share theirs." It's not evil leaders who do this—talk too much, focus on themselves, and devalue the input of those they lead. Leaders all do it to some extent. It's a human tendency. As a result, rather than sharing information that might help solve a problem, spark innovation, or avoid crises, group members say little.

We're fortunate in that some of the work we do is inside classrooms where we get to intentionally cultivate a safe climate of trust and in turn have the opportunity to ask some tough questions. Each year we teach an executive communications course at a college in southeastern Washington state. Our sections are full of adult learners—men and women putting in tough hours during the day, running home to whip up dinner for their family, and then heading across town to take one more step toward a bachelor's degree. This Speak Freely concept had been top-of-mind for us as we researched, discussed, outlined, and revised this book. One evening, we posed a question to students:

What would you like to say to your boss?

A chorus of emotionally charged answers flew at us. Some of the professionals—having lost the capacity to care—threw out things that made the entire class laugh. None of the answers seemed unreasonable. They certainly weren't mean-spirited or personal remarks. When probed as to why the students left all these things unsaid, one gentleman boldly professed, "You're asking me to choose between my ego and my livelihood!" The man genuinely feared that if he voiced his true sentiment, his boss would hold it against him until eventually showing him the door. What was the super-scary statement that this guy kept locked away in secret? "I'd like to explain that when he procrastinates, it makes my job more difficult."

He deeply wanted his boss to know this, yet the idea of actually bringing it up, he felt, would get him fired. This wasn't someone looking upward in the pecking order of an inner-city gang or distributing cocaine for a drug cartel in Central America. He toiled daily as a midlevel leader employed at a publicly traded corporation headquartered in San Francisco. But where powerful sharks swim, people refuse to become the bait.

The truth is, outside the safety of a classroom, few conversations like these take place. People hide from their leaders—all the time. We do it. You do it. The people you lead do it. But rest assured, when your people don't speak up, it's not their problem, it's yours. Leaders miss all kinds of valuable things that people keep to themselves. We believe it is the leader's responsibility to create an authentic environment, characterized by honesty and trust, that encourages everyone to share their captive thoughts and original ideas. When this happens, group members speak up and problems are solved.

Three key root causes stand between your people's thoughts and your ears:

1. The suffocating aura of your power

2. The fear of judgment and disapproval

3. Fatigue

A LEADER'S POWER
SUFFOCATES

---

*Personalities change when the President
is present, and frequently even
strong men make recommendations
on the basis of what they believe
the President wishes to hear.*

—*ROBERT F. KENNEDY*, THIRTEEN DAYS

The **USS Greenville** is a Los Angeles–class, fast-attack nuclear submarine armed with Tomahawk missiles. Commissioned in 1994, it measures 363 feet and weighs 7,177 tons.* On February 9, 2001, the sub departed for standard maneuvers off the shores of Oahu as part of a "distinguished visitor cruise"—a program intended to provide influential civilians insight into navy operations. When the *Greenville* executed an emergency main ballast tank blow nine miles shy of port, a businessman occupied the helmsman chair and a sports reporter operated valve levers. Experienced crew members supervised these guests closely while Captain Scott Waddle delivered instructions. "Emergency" main ballast blow is something of a misnomer. The procedure is pretty standard. The crew brings the submarine to periscope depth (60 feet), sweeps the area above water for other ships, and then blows out its ballast tanks to surface rapidly. Emerging from the water, a Los Angeles–class submarine looks like a giant torpedo. On this day, the *Greenville* failed to complete its rapid surface. According to the National Transportation Safety Board's (NTSB) official report:

---

*The Los Angeles class is a Naval nuclear-powered attack submarine class (SSN) that comprises more operating nuclear submarines than any other class in the world.

The guests quoted the commander as saying, "What the hell was that?" After the submarine slowed and the periscope could be raised, the CO looked into the periscope and announced that the submarine had struck another ship.[1] *

The *Ehime Maru*—a five-hundred-ton Japanese fishing boat—never had a chance. A football-field-sized projectile surfaced rapidly at 1:43 p.m., Hawaii-Aleutian Standard Time. The *Greenville* sliced the *Ehime Maru* in half, sinking it in minutes and killing nine crew members. The presence of guests complicated operations that day. Captain Waddle, the commander, and his executive officer had spent an hour of the afternoon in the captain's cabin signing photographs. Some reports suggested that Waddle had rushed the surfacing procedures because certain guests were going to be late for a meeting. The distractions undoubtedly diminished the commanding officer's situational awareness. But in the end, the NTSB cited communication issues—the failure of the crew to say anything—as the cause of the accident. Or, we might put it another way: the failure of leadership to cultivate a climate where people could speak candidly.

The National Transportation Safety Board determines that the probable cause of the collision of the *USS Greenville* with the Japanese fisheries training vessel *Ehime Maru* was the inadequate interaction and communication among senior members of the combat

---

CO is an acronym for commanding officer.

systems team (the commanding officer, the officer of the deck, the fire control technician, and the sonar supervisor), which resulted in the failure to perform adequate contact analysis and adhere to proper procedures for moving to periscope depth; and the commanding officer's decision to order an emergency surfacing maneuver.

It's difficult to speak truth to power.

Scott Waddle graduated at the top of his class from the US Naval Academy. He was a rising star with an impeccable performance record, chosen from among hundreds of qualified officers to command the *USS Greenville*. Some say there's no more intoxicating position than captain of a ship at sea. But on that day, Waddle rushed procedure at the very least. The sonar picture was murky. The commander's own periscope check (which no one wanted to question) seemed perfunctory. Critics claim that Waddle never ascended high enough with the periscope to get a true picture of traffic on the surface. For crew members, speaking up in the moment would have meant correcting the commanding officer in front of sixteen distinguished visitors. Waddle was high ranking, competent, and respected. This wasn't a case of a tyrant scowling at his subjects. This was a typical interaction between leader and followers. Only the result was extraordinary.

> Excuse me, sir, but I don't think we should surface.
> *I made the decision. Just do your job, Lieutenant.*

"The moment a leader allows himself to become the primary reality people worry about, rather than reality being the primary reality," observes Jim Collins in his book *Good to Great*, "you have a recipe for mediocrity or worse." Suddenly ending the lives of nine innocent Japanese fishermen is inarguably worse.

Professor Adam Grant of the Wharton School calls power-filled leaders takers, which he explains as people who strive to get as much as possible from others.[2] "Although group members perceive takers as highly effective leaders, takers actually undermine group performance," Grant explains. "Speaking dominantly convinces group members that takers are powerful, but it stifles information sharing, preventing members from communicating good ideas." Grant concocted a simple experiment to demonstrate the effect. He and his colleagues brought teams together to fold T-shirts. In half of the groups, leaders were instructed to speak with force and direct the group. Prior to the experiment, they even spent some time reading about the merits of extroverts. The other half did not read up on extroverts and received guidance to temper their input and lead quietly: "There are others in the group who have contributions to make," the researchers reminded them. On the teams with the quiet leaders who remained supportive and welcomed suggestions, output came in 22 percent higher. Grant points out that some may see such receptive, deferent leaders as weak. So, if looking good is your goal, we recommend talking a lot. However, if performance is your objective, we recommend you lead in a way that encourages others to speak up.

VitalSmarts, a health care development organization that has trained more than one million people worldwide, in conjunction with a couple of nursing organizations, conducted two in-depth studies of communication in health care.[3] Among other things, the studies pointed out that 58 percent of surveyed nurses admitted that "they had been in situations where it was either unsafe to speak up or they were unable to get someone to listen." Sometimes the situations are tricky, such as when an experienced doctor's incompetence threatens a patient. We can all empathize with the difficulty of voicing your thoughts in such a scenario. But others are simple:

> Each year, 1 in 20 patients at hospitals will be given a wrong medication, 3.5 million will get an infection from someone who didn't wash his or her hands or take other appropriate precautions, and 195,000 will die because of mistakes made while they're in the hospital.

The combined capacity of Yankee Stadium, the Louisiana Superdome, and CenturyLink Field in Seattle would fall fifteen hundred seats short of accommodating those who die in our medical facilities each year due to errors potentially preventable by fostering an environment where everyone speaks freely—where people can say plainly, "You forgot to wash your hands."

Instead, nurses learn to keep quiet. The report *Silence Kills* cites research on organizational communication and concludes, "Solving undiscussables will require deeper changes to cultural practices, social norms, and personal skills."[4] We don't disagree that culture creates much of the problem—culture shows new members what to say and what not to say. It's absolutely something leaders must overcome in the quest to liberate every voice. But as the leader, you shape culture. Leaders control what happens in their lane through their words, their actions, and most important, their mindset. Consider how this nurse's chilling account will shape her and her peers. She had a concern for a patient's safety, so she contacted the doctor on call:

> The surgeon was at a dinner party ... and was very vocal about how much trouble I would be in if he had to come back to the hospital for no reason. He came back and took the patient into surgery. The leg had occluded. I was never so nervous about the outcome, and was so relieved to have been correct.

This nurse was "relieved" that she was correct—so she wouldn't receive a lashing from the surgeon—even though it meant the patient was in trouble.

VitalSmarts trains low-power health care workers in skills necessary for speaking up. At the conclusion of their report, the authors portray characteristics of exceptional nurses—those who speak up fearlessly: "They begin by explaining their positive intent and use facts and data as much as possible." VitalSmarts reeducates people. It teaches them how to do what they weren't afraid to do in kindergarten. This is a necessary skill in cultures of silence. But what if leaders disposed of the nonsense, set aside ego, valued everyone's perspective, and intentionally elicited input?* Wouldn't that be easier? And smarter? And less exhausting? And more efficient?

"You'd better not interrupt my dinner party."

Seriously?

---

*Another major stumbling block is leader insecurity. It's a book in and of itself: self-awareness and self-management. Speak Freely is helpful only to those who admit that they are part of the problem (or the entire problem).

PEOPLE FEAR
JUDGMENT

*How very little can be done
under the spirit of fear.*

—FLORENCE NIGHTINGALE

Coleman County sits just under two hundred miles southwest of Dallas in the-middle-of-nowhere, Texas. On a scorching summer day in 1960-something, Jerry Harvey sat on his in-laws' porch playing dominoes on a folding card table. The temperature peaked at 104 degrees. Only a small fan, periodic wind gusts, and some cold lemonade mitigated the heat. But Jerry was nonetheless enjoying his game of dominoes, occasionally looking down at his feet to see fine grains of dust blowing across the deck and disappearing between the gaps in the floorboards.

Jerry's father-in-law cut into the peace of the Sunday afternoon by suggesting that the family take a trip to get some dinner in Abilene. "What? Go to Abilene?" Jerry thought to himself. He could hardly tolerate the idea of driving fifty-three miles back and forth in an un-air-conditioned Buick with his wife and in-laws. But before Jerry could grimace and furrow his brow, his wife chimed in: "Sounds like a great idea."

Jerry acquiesced, and then his mother-in-law voted yes by exclaiming that she hadn't been to Abilene in quite a long time. So the four family members ventured north that day based on a unanimous vote. And then Jerry's predictions of disaster came true: "The heat was brutal. We were coated with a fine layer of dust that cemented with perspiration by the time we arrived." The foursome ate a mediocre meal and raced home to seek the relief of the porch fan.

With the purr of the fan the only noise breaking a silent night, Jerry decided to be sociable. "It was a great trip, wasn't it?" At that moment, full of frustration, suddenly no one feared judgment from the others. Jerry's mother-in-law voiced her irritation. She would rather have stayed home. "I wouldn't have gone if you hadn't all pressured me into it." Apparently, not having been to Abilene "in quite a long time" was her way of suggesting that she could wait even longer. Jerry fired back by expressing his contentment with the dominoes he'd been playing. His wife, with contempt for both of them, blamed her dad and Jerry. "It wasn't my idea."

"Hell!" Jerry's father-in-law shouted. "I never wanted to go to Abilene. I just thought you might be bored." The vote-out-loud had been four to zero for the trip. The unspoken vote resoundingly favored sitting on the porch all evening. But it was far too late. The trip to Abilene was five hours of their lives that Jerry Harvey and his family would never get back. Jerry reflected in the aftermath:

> After the outburst of recrimination, we all sat back in silence. Here we were, four reasonably sensible people who, of our own volition, had just taken a 106-mile trip across a godforsaken desert in a furnace-like temperature through a cloud-like dust storm to eat unpalatable

food at a hole-in-the-wall cafeteria in Abilene, when none of us had really wanted to go.*

The Abilene Paradox is a classic. Harvey first told the story in 1974, touting "mutual agreement" as a detriment more insidious than even organizational conflict. He attributed the problems of sensible people's silence to fear: "Both research and experience indicate ostracism is one of the most powerful punishments that can be devised. . . . The fear of taking risks that may result in *judgment* from others is at the core of the paradox."† We can attribute failed family trips and disasters as monumental as the Watergate scandal to the specter of social judgment. When asked by a senator, "What on earth would it have taken to decide against the [Watergate] plan?" Jeb Magruder—a deputy to President Nixon—responded under oath, "Not very much, sir." Herbert Porter, a partner in crime and colleague on the White House staff, told the Senate panel, "I drifted along . . . in all honesty, because of the fear of the group pressure that would ensue, of not being a team player." An autopsy of America's most damaging political moment revealed

---

*We built this narrative entirely from Jerry Harvey's original work as found in *Classics of Organizational Behavior*. The notion of the Abilene Paradox is often misused in popular literature. The key to the idea is that a selected course of action must be no one's preferred option, yet the group still chooses it. It's entirely the result of individuals' failing to speak up candidly.

†We took the liberty here of replacing the word "separation" with "judgment." Both are powerful, and either fits. Harvey focused on the deep impact of social isolation. Judgment creates a form of psychological isolation from others.

that none of the players considered the Watergate break-in a good idea. The president's men went to Abilene together. We're talking about grown adults, and the diagnosis is peer pressure. These are shake-your-head moments. If fear of social disapproval weighs so mightily in the absence of significant power dynamics, imagine how strong the metaphorical winds of judgment become when powerful figures enter the mix.

The world's leading authority on psychological safety in teams, Amy Edmonson, unwraps the ways in which we prioritize our image and act to save face. People fear asking for help, admitting errors, or seeking feedback—even when it will benefit the organization—because these vulnerabilities may create an "unfavorable impression on the people who influence decisions about promotions, raises, or project assignments."[1]

We mentioned previously the original findings from Gary Stasser's murder mystery experiment: people tend to share common knowledge but are afraid of looking foolish by voicing things only they know. Or, as Edmondson points out, they may secretly fear that sharing their "proprietary" information will lessen their own value (an adult version of keeping the homework answers to yourself). Others' silence may derive from a purer intent: some are simply reluctant to look like they're showing off.

These inhibitions are common human tendencies— tendencies amplified by the stinging, critical judgment of leaders. In his book *Social Intelligence*, Daniel Goleman illustrates the neurological mechanics at work. Social threats such as "fear of a leader's judgment or of seeming stupid" in front of others prompt cortisol levels (our stress hormone) to surge.* With increased cortisol levels come anxiety and a drop in performance. Our analytical capacity, creativity, and communication all shut down.

In his book *Outliers*, Malcolm Gladwell cites a memorable fact from the annals of the airline industry: "Captains and first officers split the flying duties equally. But historically, crashes have been far more likely to happen when the captain is in the 'flying seat.'"² At first that seems to make no sense, since the captain is almost always the pilot with the most experience. But when explained, it makes all the sense in the world. Captains will *command* while first officers will *suggest* or *hint*. It's the difference between "Turn thirty degrees right" and "I think it might be wise to turn left or right if you get the chance." Planes are safer when the least experienced pilot is flying, Gladwell explains, "because it means the second pilot isn't going to be afraid to speak up." In other words, the second pilot does not fear being judged by the less experienced one.

And the other thing about judging others is, frankly, that we're just not very good at it. Let's look at some key concepts that research teaches us. Leaders start by stereotyping. For instance, if we throw out the name Shameka Williams, your brain instantly creates a picture in your head. Not a conscious decision—your brain just does it. Got the image? Now if we throw out a different name, say, Sarah West, your brain takes an entirely different snapshot. Can you see Sarah? One

---

*Goleman uses the word "teacher" and describes the scene as a classroom setting. We use "leader" here for effect.

more name—Aradhya Subramani—and yet another photo flashes in your mind's eye. It may not be a crystal-clear image, but you could describe each woman's characteristics. If next we asked you which is the stay-at-home mom, which is an IT executive at Google, and which plays in the WNBA (Women's National Basketball Association), you would answer pretty easily. You might feel like a bad person, but you wouldn't have trouble categorizing the three fictitious women. It's how our brains work—almost by necessity.*

The story continues. Imagine that Sarah approaches a bank. What does the bank look like? What color? How big? Where is it? What's the weather outside? Now that you have your mental image of Sarah and her bank, Nobel Prize–winning economist Daniel Kahneman is going to make you feel inadequate. "If an earlier sentence had been, 'They were floating gently down the river,' you would have imagined an altogether different scene"—a different sort of bank, Kahneman explains.[3]

"Sarah approaches the bank" is an ambiguous statement. But in the absence of context, your mind created specificity. Of all the people who read *Permission to Speak Freely*, only a handful will even have considered a riverbank. Absent any actual knowledge of the three women, we created context surrounding Shameka, Sarah, and Aradhya.† How we

---

*Remember: the more powerful that leaders feel, the more they tend to stereotype. Hitler—a man of immense power—turned stereotypes into a national ethos.

†We're also guessing that most people pictured a white mom, Indian IT worker, and black basketball player.

59

process these names, and our failure to consider a riverbank, are brain mechanics that replicate themselves with far more damaging ramifications every day.

One more play-along: Imagine that Shameka, Sarah, and Aradhya are the three people assigned to your *Case of the Fallen Businessman* team. How do you decide whom you should listen to in order to solve the murder? Well, the person who talks first will immediately get the status bump. The best looking of the three will have an upper hand. One of the women might mention her college degree, wear fashionable glasses, or smile kindly. A smile gains trust, but friendliness is perceived as inversely related to competence. A rounded chin also hints at questionable expertise. You will prefer Shameka because she's tall. Believe it or not, your judgment of her competence will depend on how good she is at basketball. If she's an all-star in the WNBA, the *halo effect* explains that you'll think of her as an all-star detective, as we have difficulty parsing our judgments. The way we see a person in one regard (handsome, kind, athletic) translates to how we see him or her in all regards (smart, creative, analytical).

Assuming you even let anyone else talk (since you are the all-powerful leader), the status of the person who spoke first will soon be surpassed by the woman who speaks most often. Dominating conversational airtime results in high status. But again, beware the *halo effect*. It happens fast. If Aradhya's first comment is genius, she will do no wrong for the rest of the discussion, even if she babbles incoherently the next six times she speaks. On the other hand, if Sarah's first comment seems a little off-base, you will write her off. She could bring it like Sherlock Holmes for the next twenty minutes, but your brain will not get past that first moment of nonsense. "If we see a person first in a good light," suggests the *Economist*, "it is difficult to subsequently darken that light."4 The examples of how we judge swiftly, irrationally, and often incorrectly are almost endless. Deb Gruenfeld, a professor of leadership and organizational behavior at Stanford, tells us that people evaluate others' competence in less than one-tenth of one second.*

If you—the leader in our example—are anxious about the fight you had with your best friend, watched a particularly disturbing movie the night before, or are simply hungry and impatient, your three team members will suffer. Your sour mood will crush them. And truth be told, you don't really need to listen to them anyway. *Confirmation bias*, another contributor to our poor judgment abilities as leaders, explains that *you'll be looking for input and evidence confirming what you already believe*. Poor Sarah, with her stupid first comment, has both the halo effect and confirmation bias working against her. Oh yeah, and because the above statement is emphasized (in italics), research demonstrates that you're much more likely to believe it.

Turns out leaders are also prone to bequeath higher status on those who speak more assertively. What if Shameka entered the murder mystery discussion and suggested that she was torn about whom she thought was guilty? She'd

---

*Gruenfeld speaks from a lifetime of research on the topic of body language, judgment, and power. We heard her explain this in person when she visited one of our programs.

looked at all the evidence from a number of angles and just wasn't sure. Would you value Shameka's candor? Reading this, right now, you might say, "Yes." But if Shameka were instead providing input on how to discipline an employee, which venture to fund, or whether to sell a subsidiary, you'd likely write her off as indecisive. *"Come on, Shameka. Don't tell me you're not sure. Make a decision!"* We can hardly believe we are typing this. As a past college athlete and entrepreneur in one corner, and a former military officer in the other, what are we doing espousing the virtues of muddled indecision? After years of study and investigation, we've concluded that hearing the unfiltered, authentic thoughts of those you lead is more valuable than their presentation skills.

If Aradhya digs in with a proclamation that she has zero doubt about a decision, we admire her fortitude. It's the real-world version of a Jedi mind-trick, and we can ascribe things such as the Challenger explosion and the failed launch of the Obamacare website to the detrimental effects of demanding certainty and vilifying unfettered yet authentic doubt. What if, instead, some of the most powerful words in your organization were these: *I'm not sure. I need help. I have a new idea.* What if people could just communicate what they were really thinking, without having to run it through verbal Photoshop first?

In the end, leading well is hard. There's a lot working against us, including our own minds and emotions. Our days are busy and stressed, and our jobs require that we act quickly. We need our go-to direct reports, and we don't have time for nonsense and silly ideas. But we can get better at recognizing and mitigating both our biases and the contextual factors that are influencing our judgment, especially by enabling others to speak up and call us out. Consider everything we have talked about so far, and let's tie it together with three super-enlightening bits of research related to people speaking freely.

1. Professor Gruenfeld of Stanford asserts, "Whether an argument is persuasive is rarely a reflection of its quality; many arguments aren't even heard until the right person makes them." We don't recognize our stereotypes, our halo effects, our biases, and our judgments—and we rank people (and assign them status) consciously and subconsciously. Undoubtedly you've had an experience where you've shared an idea that received little or no response. Then Mike or Amanda shares the same idea two weeks later, and Viola, the boss, suddenly think it's great.

2. Amy Cuddy of Harvard has spent years studying the dynamics of power, body language, and influence. She explains, "People make inferences of competence based on how dominant someone appears." Multiple sources of research confirm that those who talk the most, talk first, and talk assertively gain the highest status in a group. These are the supposed "right people."[5]

BUT

3. However, according to introversion guru Susan Cain, "There's zero correlation between being the best talker and having the best ideas."[6] This doesn't mean

that people who talk a lot have poor ideas; it simply means that their ideas are no better or worse than the ideas of those who say little. But, not all the people who say little are innately introverted. Many are extroverts outside of the workplace. They don't speak up because they've been suffocated by their leaders, bitten by past experiences, and frozen by the fear of judgment and disapproval. They've become de facto introverts in order to survive in their organizations. We, as leaders, are both failing to draw out ideas from our introverts and, at the same time, shutting up our extroverts.

Leaders listen to their high-status people
(and often don't even hear anyone else).

Those who talk well, early, a lot, and loudly
earn high status.

There's zero correlation between someone being a
good talker and the quality of his or her ideas.

Uh-oh.

REJECTION LEADS TO FATIGUE

The day soldiers stop bringing you their problems is the day you have stopped leading them. They have either lost confidence that you can help them or concluded you do not care. Either case is a failure of leadership.

—*COLIN POWELL*, MY AMERICAN JOURNEY

Sir Ken Robinson's brilliant presentation titled *How Schools Kill Creativity* is the most watched TED talk of all time. Over forty million people have tuned in since he delivered it in 2006. Sir Ken makes an intriguing observation: "Kids will take a chance. If they don't know, they'll have a go. Am I right? They're not afraid of being wrong." In the TED talk, Robinson speaks primarily about creativity, suggesting that corporations stigmatize mistakes. "If you're not prepared to be wrong," he argues, "you'll never come up with anything original. . . . We are educating people out of their creative capacities."

A confident kindergartner might make a better officer of the deck than a culturally conditioned navy lieutenant. The hand would shoot up, the lips would purse, and the kid would let the captain have it: "We need to go higher with the periscope." But kids become adults—adults with inhibitions, hesitations, and fears. As we grow up, or really as our hands get smacked time and again, we unlearn to say what we think and we stop sharing our ideas.

Laura Lothrop had an idea. She had lots of them. After earning her degree in education and teaching for a brief period, she spent a decade-plus raising five kids while helping her husband build a wildly successful business. There were early days when she held a Motorola cell phone in one hand (dispatching drivers to various locations) and a newborn in the other. The living room was her office, the couch was her chair, and a Playskool table was her desk. But in 2004, it all unraveled. Lothrop experienced a bitter divorce. Seemingly a hundred legal battles later, she'd lost her house, her car, and her half of the company. She prepared food at a restaurant in a casino, studied to earn a financial planning certificate, and shuttled kids to soccer, school, and their father's house.

Lothrop struck a break in fall 2011. She'd submitted an online application to work at a local retailer. Holes-in-one during Saturday golf games and winning PowerBall tickets have seemingly better odds than landing an interview via Monster.com, but she received a call. A regional manager directed stores to seek out and hire one or two "external" assistant managers. Lothrop's degree and business experience impressed the store manager, and he brought her in. A few weeks later, she started the new job. Although she had just turned fifty, she looked ahead with anticipation. The company offered ample growth potential, and she felt confident that she could contribute immediately. She earned the highest marks at a six-week training course for new managers and encouragement that she would ascend rapidly based on her leadership acumen and professionalism.

When Lothrop returned from training, one of her initial responsibilities involved resurrecting a poorly performing outdoor living section. She worked tirelessly to recruit the right people, implement proper procedures, and meet her supervisor's expectations. It was a steep climb. Most of her peers didn't appreciate an external hire coming into the mix. Lothrop's boss, Elaine, seemed to like it even less. She was downright nasty.

But knowing that this was her chance, Laura Lothrop soldiered on. She spent ample time with shoppers, listening to their issues and concerns. One developing theme involved the repotting of plants. A number of customers asked about transplanting, worried that they'd kill their vegetation in the process and thus were hesitant to attempt it. Their fears prevented them from purchasing new containers. Lothrop saw an opportunity. Her memory returned to the horticulture elective she'd taken in high school. She recalled that plants should be moved to a pot two inches larger in diameter every six months. The store could set up a small station, quickly teaching customers how to transplant safely while also informing them of the two-inch rule. The three-minute education would provide a valuable service and sell more merchandise.

Lothrop took the idea to her boss. She hoped this would be the first of many ways she could add value through creativity and innovation. She was more excited to share her idea than she'd been in a long time. What she lacked in understanding of company operations and retail practices she would compensate for through a fresh perspective and new thinking—which is exactly why the company had hired her externally in the first place. But Lothrop learned otherwise. "Just do your job," her manager told her. "Stop with the silly ideas and take care of the day-to-day." She texted her brother that afternoon, hoping he could console her. "I guess I'll just bide my time. I'm not going to make any more suggestions until I have my own store." That time never came. She left the company nine months later.*

If Laura Lothrop is your next employee, you're facing an uphill battle earning her trust. It will be a while before she brings up an area needing improvement, raises her hand with a new idea, or admits that she doesn't quite understand. Her last boss—and the culture of her last organization—taught her to put her head down and just do her job. Millions of creative, intelligent, and eager people are living out their lives in the same way all around us. And inside almost every one of them are ideas that can change your organization for the better.

The people you lead have likely never encountered Laura Lothrop's boss, but someone, somewhere, robbed them of their eagerness to contribute. We shared Lothrop's story during a session with midlevel leaders at a large company. When done, we asked if anyone had examples of similar experiences. Many hands slowly ascended, and a gentleman in the front row raised his hand and sheepishly began to share. He'd spent his entire career in finance, but one day his boss assigned him a complex marketing project. She told him to attack the task but knew it was not his area of expertise. "If you get stuck," she assured him, "if you need any help, just let

---

*We later shared this story with a vice president at the company. Before we could deliver the punch line that Lothrop had been shut down, the executive proclaimed, "That's a great idea. We could get the vendors to pay for the station and sell more merchandise."

me know. Worst case—if it's simply beyond your scope—we can assign it to someone else. But I'd like you to try."

The executive battled the marketing project for two weeks, but he floundered.

> I just didn't have the ability to do it well. I'm a finance guy and it was a marketing project—and an important one. So I went to my boss, and I told her I needed help—told her I thought it would be better if someone else took the lead. She paused for a moment, then looked right at me and declared in a harsh tone, "You never say that around here. Never tell people you can't do something. Say that around here, and it'll get around. Your career will be over." I learned never to speak up around here again. I just keep my mouth shut.

From that moment forward, what was best for the organization became subordinate to his fears of asking for help or admitting he needed assistance. His own boss—the leader charged with answering his questions, providing him guidance, and developing his talents—instead became a predator lurking in the tall grass.

PART THREE

HOW TO CULTIVATE A CULTURE OF CANDOR

ASSUME POSITIVE INTENT

If someone doesn't trust you, it doesn't matter how well you measure your words, the other person will misinterpret you. If someone trusts you implicitly, it doesn't matter how poorly you phrase something, the other person will assume you meant well.

—BRUCE BROWN, FOUNDER, PROACTIVE COACHING

Forging a culture of candor—one where people share their questions and uncertainties, their good and bad ideas, and their feedback and concerns—turns on one thing: positive intent. It is what holds everything else together—the center of gravity. You grant those you lead permission to speak freely under the condition that they say anything and everything for the good of the organization and those who are a part of it. This is an effect rather than a capability. We are not suggesting that people must be capable enough to have a positive impact; we are arguing that this must be their *intent*.

When Steven Hauschka suggested that the Seahawks not kick a field goal, it was requisite that he said so intending to help the team win the game.

When a junior officer tells the captain of a submarine to do another periscope sweep . . .

When a mother-in-law admits that she doesn't want to go to Abilene . . .

When Laura Lothrop suggests a display teaching people how to transplant their garden foliage . . .

When a nurse reminds, "Wash your hands . . ."

… it must all be said with positive intent. And while much of what we teach as leader developers hinges on the idea "Leadership is not about you," this, in fact, is all about you. As a leader, you must create this positive intent. You must, or none of this will work. How do you do that? How in the world do you get every single person in your organization to speak out loud with the greater good in mind? How, as a leader, can you possibly create positive intent in those you lead?

It's simple.

You assume it.

Simple, yet one of the hardest things you will ever do. For most leaders, this will require a significant change in mindset. And real, sustainable change in the way we think takes immense effort and often a long time. Shann Ferch, the psychologist and professor at Gonzaga University who wrote the foreword to this book, requires potential clients to commit to a two-year minimum plan before he will take them on, citing psychological research that shows it takes two to five years for new behaviors to fully set in and become character changes. Hence the common notion in psychology, *fake it until you make it.* "Through a combination of humility, gracefulness, and grit, people who commit to the two to five years for character changes most often succeed in achieving those changes," Ferch explains. "People too attached to their egos and unwilling to submit to the crucible of change don't change."*

---

*Ferch is a top-tier professor and colleague, and he provided us with this direct quote. We have heard him teach these lessons on personal change several times when he has been a guest speaker for our leadership programs.

For Doug Crandall, everything he did as a leader changed on a fall day in the basement of West Point's Thayer Hall. Doug connected with Everett Spain to discuss teacher development for the next summer's cohort of incoming faculty. Major Everett Spain was a leader among leaders, doing all the little things right, like grabbing the smallest corner office on purpose. As Spain saw it, leaders "eat" last.* He had run the process the previous year, and Doug would be leading the charge in June. The Faculty Development Workshop (FDW) was a crash course in West Point's core leadership offering: PL300. Doug and his colleagues spent six weeks as students of every fifty-five minute lesson they would soon teach. When August rolled around, they were handed the conch, and each of them taught four practice lessons on transformational leadership, culture, power, and influence, or any number of topics. During the practice classes, the experienced faculty role-played students. Some of them asked cynical questions, pretended to fall asleep, talked too long, and shuffled their books and papers prematurely as the end of class approached. Cadets at West Point are committed and bright for the most part, but they are still college students. The experienced teachers were trying to get the new faculty ready. Spain and Doug were debating the merits of this role-playing tradition when Spain raised his voice slightly and declared, "I hate that stuff! I hate it!"

Everett Spain is a real-life version of Forrest Gump (except he's the genius version). His life almost ended during US

---

*Simon Sinek used this phrase as the title of a best-selling book. The idea has been a central artifact of military culture for decades.

Army Ranger School when hypothermia brought his heart-beat to a halt. A Blackhawk helicopter flew him to the closest emergency room, and medical personnel revived him. After his engineer company won the prestigious Draper Award as the best unit in Europe, Spain studied business at Duke and returned to West Point to teach. He became the first (and only) academic faculty member to receive a Purple Heart, after he stepped down from his teaching post to deploy to Iraq in 2004 and was struck by shrapnel. Spain later worked as a White House Fellow, was promoted early to colonel, and earned his PhD at Harvard, where he won the highest peacetime medal for valor while acting as an impromptu first responder during the Boston Marathon bombing. He's now back at West Point (in a bigger office) as the head of the leadership department.

So there Doug sat in fall 2003, startled by Spain's procla-mation that he hated the role-playing stuff. *Is this just Ever-ett being Everett?* Doug thought to himself.

"Why, Everett? Why do you hate that stuff?"

"I hate it," he continued, "because I have never met a bad cadet. Never. We teach our new faculty that they fall asleep, wield cynical tongues, and act like slackers. We set up those expectations. But I mean it—I've never met a bad one. They are all trying to do the right thing."

Doug doesn't remember when he decided to experiment with Everett Spain's view of the world. It was not right away. Doug left Spain's office mocking him a bit. *Never met a bad cadet. Yeah. Whatever.* But then he decided to visit a few of Spain's classes. No one slept, no one shuffled papers, and no one asked cynical questions. Spain's body language beamed

respect for his students. There was a vibrant, intelligent dialogue in his classrooms. You could step out of his room a
few feet into the hall and look through windows into other
classes. There were glazed-over looks, signs of fear, and hints
of quiet desperation. And then—boom! You popped back
into Spain's PL300 lesson and hands were in the air, students
were debating how to best motivate others, and Spain was
standing in the corner watching them thrive.

He had been living out one of the very concepts he was
teaching: a scientifically proven phenomenon called the Pygmalion Effect, with roots that extend back half a century. It
suggests that *our mere beliefs about others have a causal impact
on their attitudes, actions, and performance.* Scott Snook, a
retired army colonel and Harvard PhD who was instrumen-
tal in the transformation of West Point's leader development
system at the turn of the century, asserts, "The Pygmalion
Effect is the most underappreciated experiment in psychology, and the one with the most powerful implications for
leaders."*

If you cringe at the spectacle of lab rats being treated like
lab rats, you won't like this story. But it's an enlightening
introduction to the narrative of understanding how assuming intent creates intent. In 1966, J. R. Burnham injected some
ingenuity into a developing school of research: exploring

---

*Snook is a brilliant teacher. He now leads efforts to develop and
deliver authentic leadership courses as a senior lecturer at Harvard
Business School.

how the preconceptions of experimenters impacted the final results of an experiment. Previous studies had demonstrated conclusively that if lab workers believed their rats were "gifted," the animals performed better on a series of maze navigations. The supervisors provided the supposedly superior rodents with more physical handling, more encouragement, and less corrective feedback. Yes, we are talking about rats, the things with tails that when not in a laboratory live in dark alleys and sewers.

Burnham wanted to up the game. He had a number of experimenters put the rats through a maze exercise. About half of the rats underwent a brain-cortex removal surgery. Some of the others received a "sham" surgery, where Burnham produced a slight head wound but did not remove the cortex. Overwhelmingly, the best performers in the maze were the rats whose "leaders" believed that their brains were fully operational—had a cortex—and whose brains in fact did have a cortex. Not surprising.

© Robert Adrian Hillman

However, if a rat's brain cortex had not been removed, but the experimenter believed it had because of the slight head wound, performance dropped dramatically. It decreased almost to the same level as that of the rats who actually had their cortex taken out. (And as you probably guessed, even if an experimenter believed that his or her rat's brain was intact, this could not overcome the absence of a cortex.)

This experiment teaches us, in essence, that as long as the people you lead have a functioning brain, assuming positive intent will yield the best results—by a landslide. Later that same year (1966), Robert Rosenthal of Harvard connected with a San Francisco Bay Area educator, Lenore Jacobson. The two decided to research human subjects and determine if preconceptions about a student's learning ability would impact actual intellectual development. Their resulting work became oft-cited support for this notion that our beliefs about others have a causal impact.

Rosenthal and Jacobson found this to be true at the Oak Hill School. Students whose teachers had been conditioned to believe they were on the precipice of an academic burst experienced a surge. Teachers evaluated this group as more interesting, more affectionate, more adjusted, and destined for a more successful future. However, just as researchers had convinced experimenters that they had the "gifted" rats (nonsense), so too were the students in the Oak Hill experiment selected randomly. The experiment at Oak Hill overwhelmingly demonstrated an impact on in-class behavior.[1]

Dov Eden, a professor at Israel's Tel Aviv University, took the line of research to new heights. In 1982, Eden gained access to an Israeli Defense Forces (IDF) combat command course. The IDF permitted Eden and a colleague to condition four military instructors with information similar to what was used in the lab rat experiments of the mid-1960s: a number of the command course participants were classified as *high CP* (Command Potential), others were designated as *regular CP*, and some were identified with a question mark (unclassifiable). Just as in the lab rat experiment, this was complete nonsense; the designations were entirely random. The inclusion of an unclassifiable category added to the legitimacy of the ruse. Its intent was to eliminate any suspicion on the part of the four instructors.

Seven weeks later, the results were in. The *high CP* soldiers substantially outperformed their peers. "The differences in performance evidenced a substantial Pygmalion Effect," Eden concluded, "about 15 points on a conventional 100 points grade scale." Eden drew some conclusions, which everyone on the planet who leads another human being should absorb:

> The instructors were quite good leaders for those of whom they expected a lot, but not good leaders of those from whom they expected less.... If managers would treat all their subordinates to the same quality of leadership that they lavish upon those of whom they expect the most, all would perform better.[2]

And there you have it. Dov Eden reduced his years of research to a simple conclusion: *Leaders get what they expect—* be it success in a maze, behavior in a classroom, performance in a training program, or positive contributions from their people. A bit of good news is that this entire notion is made easier (although not easy) by the fact that we, as leaders, get to set expectations. We can create positive, lofty visions for our people and help them to achieve, or choose to view them as average and remain status quo. It's our choice.

Dov Eden is an eclectic academic. He's known as one of the world's leading authorities on the impacts of vacation time. Not a bad gig. He concocted further iterations of the IDF experiment. He found that the Pygmalion Effect works both ways—positively and negatively.[3] The negative side has been dubbed the Golem Effect.* If we believe that our people are lazy, dumb, dull, or any number of negatives, we create those results. Eden also demonstrated the Pygmalion Effect on a group level. In different IDF courses, instructors were led to believe certain things about their entire platoon. Same results. Leaders got what they expected.

Eden admits that there's a central element to the Pygmalion Effect research: the leaders and followers are unwitting participants. The instructors in the Israeli Defense Force experiment didn't know it was all made up. They truly believed that certain soldiers in the unit had high command potential. Scott Snook explained it to us this way: "The one thing you can do—that's totally in your power—is you can decide what to look for in those you lead." You must truly believe that your people are capable—whether they do or not. When a fourth-grade teacher believes that she has a "gifted" student, everything works a bit differently. It's in the attribution that the teacher makes. If the student with an asterisk of excellence next to his name fails a test, what's the teacher's assumption? *Hmmm . . . I must have let him down. He's too smart to fail.* With no asterisk, our default

_____

*Golem is the Hebrew word for "dumbbell."

assumption differs. *He must not have studied. He's just not that smart. He just doesn't care.* It's the same with a comment, suggestion, or critique.

When Everett Spain told Doug that he'd never met a bad cadet, he didn't take Doug to a whiteboard and illustrate the fundamentals of Dov Eden's research. He didn't mention any lab rats. He wasn't trying to convince Doug of anything at all (other than to dispense with the role-playing in the faculty development process). Major Spain stated plainly: "I've never met a bad cadet." *He believed it, and that's the key.*

Following Spain's lead, Doug made a conscious decision at the outset of his second semester to never meet a bad cadet. A few days into January, a cadet arrived late to one of the morning sections. When a student shows up tardy in Thayer Hall, he has to knock on the door (calling attention to himself in front of fifteen classmates), render a salute, and announce: "Sir, Cadet Harris reports late to class." The old Doug would have saluted back and fired a few brain neurons wondering where the cadet had been. *He probably overslept, doesn't care about my class, and won't pay attention while he's here.* It's that fast, and then it's back to teaching before the student even sits down. The post–Everett Spain Doug chose to process it all differently. When the cadet knocked on the door and announced that he was late, Doug smiled at him and thought: *Must have a good reason; some other officer probably kept him late.* The thoughts that run through a leader's head have a causal impact on the people being led—influencing the way they behave and perform.

For the next four and a half years, Doug's students were great—every single one of them. The cadets hadn't changed.

He had. He even got a little countercultural, telling his students not to knock on the door when they were late. "I know you have a good reason. Just come in and sit down." Did he truly know they had a good reason? Probably not. But he never worried about it. He just assumed they did. Maybe some of them got one over on him occasionally, but it was worth it. The incredibly positive upside of thinking this way paid enormous dividends. The longer he lived out his leadership believing he'd never meet a bad cadet, the more real it became. His classes started to look less like summer practice sessions and more like Everett Spain's.

In these teaching experiences at West Point, Doug had been able to shift his mind-set to one where every student he encountered was a good one. Later, he took this view of others with him in other professional roles, and he was now coaching youth basketball this way. Then he put the notion to the mightiest of tests. As he stepped out of his black Honda Accord and gazed through a chain-link fence topped with barbed wire, he whispered a short prayer: "Lord, help me to never meet a bad prisoner." He thought he might need a bit of divine intervention to assume positive intent inside the confines of a medium-security prison.

Everything about getting to the classrooms at Coyote Ridge Corrections Center was a reminder that these guys were bad. There were uniformed guards, metal detectors, ID checks, and powerful electronic doors that slid ominously open and closed. Once through the maze of doors and fences, Doug emerged into an open prison yard. He wondered, *When I get through this secure area, do I really just go outside all by myself?* There were a couple of "offenders" a hundred feet in front of him, walking a medium-sized dog. A goateed and tattooed man in drab clothing came toward him pushing some sort of cart. Doug diligently moved on, picked up his pace, and headed for the education building.

Doug's first class was better, and worse, than he'd imagined. The better part was that everything seemed pretty community college-ish from an academic perspective. There was a lab full of computers, every classroom had a whiteboard, and the course enrollments were manageable at about twenty. It was worse in that he found out quickly that these guys ran the gamut from murder-one to armed robbery to extortion to drunk driving. He knew his thoughts would drive his actions and ultimately create either a Pygmalion or Golem effect—one or the other. On paper, this was the toughest positive-intent test yet.

There were several guys—Nate Corbray, Daniel Shea, Nick Bunn, Silas Robbins, and Jermal Joe—who rose to the top of the class as the semester went on. Two others, Percy Levy and Dave Walker, were total standouts. Levy was born in a prison—literally. His mom had been locked up in a New Mexico correctional facility during his conception (apparently conjugal visits are real things), during his birth, and every single year of his life until she was released when Percy was ten. *Finally,* he thought, *I get the chance to have a mom like everyone else.* Except Percy's mom wasn't like everyone else's. Just a few days after she picked up little Percy from his twenty-third foster home, she beat the hell out of him. That became habit. The woman who gave birth to Percy—the one who was supposed to read him Dr. Seuss and make him peanut better and jelly sandwiches—instead used kitchen knives to stab him in the arm. "I'd describe the things that were done to me when I was younger," Levy said a few years later at his graduation from the education program, "but they are so brutal it's best I leave them to your imagination. That being said, your imagination will never do them justice."

Levy earned an A+ in speech class. Yet no one in the world had ever believed in Percy Levy. No one. Not a single person on this planet of seven billion had ever heard a word come out of his mouth and assumed that he was coating it with some sort of positive intent. The "joke" below was part of a training program that new faculty members are required to attend in preparation to teach at Coyote Ridge—an annual requirement for everyone who works in the Washington State Department of Corrections.

Q: How do you know if a prisoner is lying?
A: His lips are moving.

Put another way, every year, the Department of Corrections reminds every employee that all these guys do is lie—all the time. They are also taught that prisoners are always trying to manipulate them, and they need to be on the defensive. We're pretty sure that these aren't official parts of the curriculum, but culture is rarely about what's official.

To be sure, Percy Levy has a chip on his shoulder the size of a ball and chain. He is a cynical, large, sometimes angry man who often glares at people. But Percy Levy is also something else—utterly brilliant.

The other person who stood out was David Walker. He is tall, bald, and slender, and he doesn't glare like Levy. From what we understand, Levy committed some armed robberies and left a few people badly beaten. David Walker sold drugs too many times. He sold drugs so that he could buy drugs. "I was a junkie," Walker told us. "Finally my counselor had enough. I remember standing there in court and she tells the judge, 'Mr. Walker has hit bottom, furnished it, moved in, and is living there comfortably.'"

Three-strikes-and-you're-out landed David Walker a double-digit sentence. He's had plenty of time to make meaning of his life story:

> I remember when I was nineteen. I was working the
> graveyard shift at a meat-cutting factory. Guys would
> get off work and take me to bars—drinking, getting
> high, and doing cocaine. One morning I wake up
> and I'm late for something. I go running through the
> kitchen past my dad. He almost never talked to me.
> He wasn't even there for the first nine years of my life.
> All of a sudden on Valentine's Day in 1973 he shows up
> and proposes to my mom. I really didn't know what to
> think of him. But he grabs me in the kitchen this day
> and spins me around a bit. He points at me and snick-
> ers with disgust, "When you are forty, you are going to
> wake up alone and with nothing."

On his fortieth birthday, Dave Walker woke up alone and with nothing, locked behind thick metal bars in a cold room on a prison bed. His dad's words bounced back and forth like a pinball inside his head. He has a flashbulb memory of that moment in the kitchen. He can see himself spinning around and catching the disapproving gaze of his father. The short scene kept replaying in his mind that birthday morning and he simply started to cry. Two years later, Dave Walker stood at his mother's funeral in shackles and an orange jumpsuit. His dad had died a year before that, but he hadn't bothered to attend the service.

After teaching at the facility for nearly three years, Doug asserted with every ounce of sincerity: "I never met a bad prisoner." What changed him as leader at West Point carried over to teaching at the prison. To be sure, we're not touting Doug's prowess as a leader. Rather, we're simply explaining that when he changed the way he thought, everything around him changed with it. Everything. If your people are going to *speak freely*—if you plan to reap the incredible benefits of everyone you lead being candid—you must never again meet a "bad cadet."

The two of us (Doug and Matt) team-taught an honors class at Coyote Ridge as our final course there, developing it as a way to give the best inmates something positive in their lives. We limited attendance to fifteen. In order to gain a spot in the class, inmates needed a GPA of 3.5 or higher, could have had no disciplinary infractions during the previous 365 days, and had to write a one-page essay explaining why they belonged in the course. More than one hundred men applied. Being dubbed the "best of the best"—for the first time in their lives—had limitless power. Men cried. We spent a ten-week quarter with these guys. There were guest speakers, leadership philosophy papers, and some of the best dialogue we'd ever experienced in a classroom. Percy Levy and David Walker were two of the top students.

Levy said a few harsh things in class. Every time he released anger, though, we assumed that it came from a good place—maybe a desire to be understood. We still hear from him via an email system called JPay, and his wife is a Facebook friend. He's earned more privileges via good behavior, and since finishing his community college program with honors, he's published four fiction books. They are urban tales, salty and real. He's actually told us a couple of times not to read them. Despite the bond we formed, there's still a part of Levy that fears our judgment. You, however, can find his books on Amazon right now. Seriously. Just search for Percy Levy.*

Dave Walker earned his associate's degree and is only a few credits away from finishing a bachelor's at Ohio University. He's done it all via snail mail. Walker is one of our favorite people. We still correspond with him and give him reading recommendations. In addition to his college work, we told him to study *Primal Leadership*, by Daniel Goleman; *Multipliers*, by Liz Wiseman; *Organizational Culture and Leadership*, by Edgar Schein; and *Difficult Conversations*, by Douglas Stone, Bruce Patton, Sheila Heen, and Roger Fisher.† He read them all and sent a mini-recap of each. Along with one of his reports, he included a long letter. One thing stood out in his writing. David Walker was speaking freely—discussing his postconfinement plans and suggesting that he could become a world-class leader developer (with an amazing backstory).

Power, rejection and fatigue, or fear of judgment could get in the way of a dream that big. Walker spoke it. It's our

---

Slave to the Trade series and *Urban Love* series.
†All outstanding books relating to leadership and leader development.

job as leaders to dignify the try and empower those we lead to say what's on their minds and in their hearts. Even inside a medium-security prison, assuming positive intent worked to create positive intent. A group of armed robbers, murderers, and drug dealers moved past the muzzles that had been part of their required dress code and started to speak freely. We could have taken our honors leadership course participants, put them in khakis and button-downs, and placed them in a section at Harvard Business School. No one would have known the difference.

We placed Bruce Brown's quote at the outset of this chapter with the assurance that it's exactly where it belongs. Go look at it again. What we hear as leaders is not about the words—it's never really about the words. It comes down to how we perceived the messengers' intent. Of course Steven Hauschka wanted to win that NFC Championship game. Seahawks coach Pete Carroll could have inferred self-doubt, weakness, selfishness, or even cowardice from Hauschka's comments. Instead, he assumed positive intent. When a nurse says, "Remember to wash your hands," a doctor can assume that she's on a power trip, doesn't like him, or enjoys nagging people. Or, he can assume that she cares about her patients. The research we shared earlier on silence in hospitals drew a conclusion about the courageous nurses who speak up successfully: "They begin by explaining their positive intent."

Here's what we are suggesting: Never, ever make anyone explain it. Just assume it. We can't state the case more strongly: *You get what you expect.* Assuming positive intent has worked with rats, middle-school students, Israeli military officers, West Point cadets, youth basketball players, and convicted felons. Don't send thousands of nurses, deck officers, field-goal kickers, and assistant managers to communication training. Instead, create positive intent throughout your organization—by assuming it. This doesn't happen on the margins; it happens person by person with *everyone* you lead. And it will undoubtedly feel awkward at first, but if you commit to shifting your mind-set to assume that those you lead have the best of intentions when they say things— even the "wrong" things in the "wrong" way—you're on the path to creating a climate where everyone has *permission to speak freely*.

Before you read any further, stop for a moment and ponder: What's *your* own mind-set about the intent and motivation of those you lead? What do you choose to believe? What do your words and body language say to others? And finally, are you willing to commit to the hard work of making everybody around you better, by submitting to a new perspective?

PROVE IT'S SAFE

Vulnerability is not weakness. . . .
Vulnerability is our most accurate
measurement of courage.

—BRENÉ BROWN, TED TALK, MARCH 2012

During the summer after his junior year of college, Matt Kincaid decided to take on a College Pro Painters franchise in an attempt to earn more money than the measly $2,500 he had earned during previous summer jobs. He knew a guy who had earned $14,000 one summer doing this, which was plenty of incentive to give it a try. He learned the ins and outs of the business and hired nine college students to work for him, including his friend Seth. He'd known Seth since the eighth grade and trusted him immensely. Seth quickly became the foreman for one of the three crews.

All summer Matt did everything he could to stay a week or two ahead of his workers, providing estimates to anyone who would listen. He even paid cute college girls to knock on neighborhood doors, smile and flirt with whoever answered (hopefully a young guy), and solicit more estimates. When he wasn't giving estimates, he was painting alongside his crews. He didn't sleep much, regularly putting in fifteen-hour days, but running a business for the first time was exhilarating.

Fast-forward six years. Matt and Seth were in their midtwenties, playing in a summer league basketball game with a group of guys. Basketball had always brought them together. Of all the friends they had, nobody loved the game more than the two of them. They restructured their schedules routinely to meet up and shoot hoops together, sometimes even playing at midnight if it meant they could sneak into a gym somewhere for an hour. As the game ended, Seth asked, "Hey Matt, can I talk to you for a second?" "Of course. What's up?"

Seth was a pretty quiet guy, always carried himself calmly, and rarely said anything negative. Matt simply figured he was having girlfriend trouble or something similar, so without concern, he looked at Seth and awaited his response. "Something has been bothering me for a long time . . ." Seth paused. "Do you remember that house we painted in Pullman for the old lady who lived off the dirt road?" The statement immediately flashed a picture of the house in Matt's mind. They had painted only three houses in Pullman that summer, and only one had been for a woman who lived off a dirt road. "Yeah, I remember," he responded curiously. Seth asked, "Why didn't we use that special primer on the foundation of her house to kill all the moss like you told her we would?"

Matt squinted and stared at Seth, his mind spinning. It hadn't occurred to him that they had neglected to use the appropriate primer, but the thought of it quickly reminded him of the conversation with the woman. He remembered the upstairs living room in the aged split-entry home where they sat on her 1950s furniture and recalled her expressing concern over the moss. He visualized her kind, wrinkled face as she smiled and signed the contract. He felt a pit in his stomach. "I don't know. I must have forgotten."

Years later as we were discussing writing this book, the conversation with Seth kept surfacing. Matt recalled thinking at the time that he was doing a pretty good job as a leader of the painting company. His employees seemed to like working for him, he had empowered them with autonomy and freedom, and he constantly looked for small ways to reward them. Yet he had failed as a leader in two crucial ways. First, and obviously, he had failed the client. He had promised the woman something he and his crew didn't deliver on. And certainly he had shown up and collected her money as the crew loaded up their drop cloths and ladders and moved on to the next job.

But second, he had failed Seth. He was unaware that his power as the leader had hindered Seth from speaking up at a moment that mattered—at a moment when a mistake was being made and their integrity was at stake. Matt had not been intentional enough about ensuring that the lines of communication were open, and Seth clearly did not feel he could speak freely. Even worse, it was several more years before Seth mustered the courage to approach Matt in an attempt to clear his conscience.

Speaking freely about primer or moss in the moment would have rendered a better result. At minimum, Seth would not have been stuck carrying the burden of guilt around for years. And more than likely, Matt would have simply purchased the correct product for the job and delivered on his promise to the client. This action also would have reinforced the notion of speaking freely to Seth, thereby encouraging even more candor in the future. Summoning the bravery to talk about using the correct primer on a house was not something Seth should ever have had to do. It should have flowed out of his mouth without a second thought. And if Matt had been more intentional about cultivating an intentional culture within the small group, reminding everyone that they could—and should—voice any idea or concern that ever crossed their minds, it likely would have.

But none of this happened. As a leader, you must learn how to recognize the hindrances to open communication. It's not enough to encourage people once in a while and have an open-door policy. You must explicitly tell your people that they can speak freely to you, and you must constantly reinforce this message. Often during the two years we researched and wrote this book, we questioned each other on how we could possibly pull this off—this cultivating candor thing. But there's one thing Matt could have done differently. He wasn't a power-wielding dictator, but he didn't do enough to prove it was safe. He should have said to Seth explicitly:

> You can speak freely to me. I sincerely mean it.
>
> Say anything.
>
> Anytime.

And he should have said it often, constantly reinforcing the message.

Make your appreciation for candor explicit to those you lead. Don't assume that they know you value it. Don't assume that they know it's okay not to know. Say it. Say it tomorrow—even if you're not quite sure you believe in it yet. And once you've made the statement, follow it up with every fiber of who you are and how you behave. At times, you must even make yourself smaller in stature if you expect to hear ideas and feedback, as a leader's expressions of power muzzle people. When a computer server crashes and you need the team to act quickly, stand in front of the room and command the situation. But when you're breaking down performance from the previous quarter and asking for input on how the team can do better, choose a seat near the middle of the circle, hunch over a bit, and smile. *You must skillfully toggle between directing the group in moments of execution and becoming just another member of the team in moments of learning and discovery.*

Remi Hajjar—a stellar instructor that Doug taught with at West Point—was a master at facilitating discussions. Sometimes the instructors would tape their classes as a learning exercise to improve their teaching. He showed Doug one time how class participation dropped when he stood in front of the room. It would pick up drastically when he took a seat among the students. Such a simple shift in the power dynamic—subjugating his position of authority—encouraged people to speak up.

Making it loud and clear—both verbally and nonverbally—is simply the first step. You will inevitably have to do much more. If you're leading the gentleman from finance we mentioned earlier who took on the marketing project—the one whose boss had told him to seek help if he struggled and then belittled him when he asked—your words will ring hollow. Your direct proclamation may even kindle cynicism within those who've heard it all before. You must start by telling them that it's safe—that they can speak freely—and then you will have to prove that it's safe to all those who have been burned in the past or just don't believe.

The most compelling way to demonstrate that the waters of candor are safe is to dive in yourself. When you are the formal leader—the person with the legitimate power—you forge fearlessness in others when you demonstrate your humanity and speak vulnerably. The following is a story about one of our colleagues doing just this.

James Cameron spent five years building Walmart's Leadership Academy before the company promoted him to vice president and asked him to tackle global optimization of all its leader development.* Cameron had grown up a bit of a rebel. He got kicked out of school when he was sixteen. He never attended college. And as a young lieutenant in the British Army, he almost earned a court-martial for driving his car across a military post at reckless speeds. He's no fan of pomp, and thus no fan of the Royal Family concept, but he'll occasionally mention meeting the queen to receive his Commander of the Order of the British Empire award.† Cameron did some brilliant work as the head of counterterrorism for the UK. He understands global issues and politics as well as anyone on the planet. When he speaks about Middle Eastern conflict, dictators in Latin America, or extremism in Eastern Europe, executives at Walmart soak it all up—appreciating the chance to further their understanding of an increasingly global economy.

---

*Not *that* James Cameron (of *Titanic* and *Avatar* fame).
†CBE: one rung below knighthood.

Cameron sometimes goes out of his way to sound smart. He has a sharp wit, a short temper, and a small corner in his heart reserved for his insecurities. Never did his team trust him more than when he pulled up a chair in a small circle and admitted, "I think I'm as smart as anyone. But I live in constant fear of people's judgment because I don't have a college degree. I compensate for it quite a bit actually, and it can get in my way. It's something I really need to overcome." The team later watched Cameron admit this to a group of forty aspiring company vice presidents. Those were deep, dark waters he jumped into with that admission. According to Geoff Webb, one of Cameron's direct reports, *"We never trusted him more or felt closer to him than when he shared that part of himself."*

Vulnerability begets trust. Make yourself vulnerable—and prove it's safe for others to speak freely in your direction—through what you're willing to say and the attitude of humility with which you say it. Amy Edmondson, a professor mentioned earlier in the book as an expert on leader-follower communication, backs up this idea:

> Leaders must facilitate vital interpersonal exchanges by creating a climate of psychological safety in which it's expected people will speak up and disagree. A basic way to create such a climate is to model the behaviors: acknowledging ignorance about a topic or area of expertise, and conveying awareness of one's own fallibility.[1]

Get everyone on board with the idea that divergence of thought is a virtue—agreement that disagreement is a good thing when done with positive intent. Inspire this perspective by being vulnerable enough that others trust you. No one on James Cameron's team cared that his team lacked a college degree. His substantial intellect was self-evident. But every one of them expressed heightened regard for Cameron upon hearing his courageous admission. They knew—in that moment—that their boss was willing to speak freely to them, and they began to believe that reciprocation would prove safe.

You've *told them* explicitly . . .

You're *sitting in the middle* of meetings as opposed to at the head of the table . . .

You've worked on establishing *welcoming body language* . . .

You're even saying you're sorry, occasionally *admitting that you don't know*, and opening up a bit . . .

Yet many of your people *still aren't sure* it's safe.

There's one final step you can take: *rope off a small boundary area*. An allegory came out of the latter half of the last century that we've seen referred to several times as the product of a "social science study." We've been strongly committed to solid research throughout this book but admit openly that we could find no actual academic support for what we're about to share. Nevertheless, it paints a nice picture of a story we will tell about a friend named Seth (a different Seth than in the painting story).

In the 1970s, social psychologists suggested that educational practices were suffocating young learners. Experts looked inside and outside the classroom for ways to provide children with freedom and room to discover. One experiment involved recess. A school district volunteered to test a fence-free playground. Researchers theorized that taking the fence down would encourage children to wander farther from the swing sets and slides to explore new turf. So they selected a school and removed the fence. Before the boundary came down, kids spent recess at the edges of the area. Certainly, some would stay close to the jungle gyms at the center of the playground, but others stood near the fence corners and did things like make up new handshakes.

When the fence was removed for the experiment, behavior changed significantly, but not as expected. The kids who had skirted the boundary no longer had any idea where they could venture to and still be "safe." All the kids retreated to the center of the playground area. Although surprising, the results were profound nonetheless: *The fence made it safe and actually enhanced risk-taking.*

When we first began writing this book, we spoke to our (other) friend Seth about the content. He was a fairly new high school ministry director at a large suburban church. He'd asked for advice on getting people to open up at team meetings. He was an energetic and bold leader—possibly hampered by his own small doses of sarcasm and a dry wit. Like most people who take on a new role, Seth had lots of ideas. The team, however, liked the status quo. Sometimes they would all just look at him when he asked for input at team meetings.

As we talked more, Seth revealed one thing he just didn't want to hear: members of his team compared him with his predecessor. He didn't want to hear input prefaced with: "Well, the way Ike used to do it was . . ." We recommended that Seth put up a fence—let those he led know that it wasn't a good idea to go over "there," but the team was free to venture absolutely anywhere else. Seth had a sincere desire to hear his people speak freely. He wanted to hear everything, with one exception. It was a perfect opportunity to prove it was safe, and the feedback he received increased significantly.

Make it explicit: I want to hear everything you have to say. Speak freely . . .

Jump in yourself: I admit that I'm insecure about how good Ike was at this job. He's a hard act to follow.

Rope off a boundary: So I really do want to hear all your thoughts and ideas, with one exception: please don't tell me how Ike used to do it. Other than that, speak freely.

When you do this effectively and people start to trust you, be ready to assume positive intent, because you will hear things that sting. It's excruciating emotional work at times. You must assume positive intent, and then you must lead. Listening to the most candid thoughts of your people—and thanking them for their input—requires true belief in the call of leadership. These commitments to the hard work of serving others will distinguish the person (leader) from the

title (boss). In writing this book, we've received some strik-
ingly candid feedback:

> "Some of your stories look like you're puffing your own
> chests as leaders."

> "I didn't get at all where you were going with that story . . .
> you lost me and I had a hard time coming back."

> "Not at all the right place for humor."

> "You seriously need to rewrite that entire chapter. It's a
> mess."

When the candid thoughts start to pour in, the unfiltered words of those you lead will challenge your heart and
mind. We must prove to those we lead that ideas will not be
mocked, candor will not incur wrath, and it's safe to jump
into the water. These steps we've shared are merely building
blocks. But you must start here, then be excited when someone makes the slightest comment or shares even an odd,
unsolicited idea. You must celebrate every toe in the water.

DIGNIFY
EVERY TRY

---

*Great spirits have always experienced
violent opposition from mediocre minds.*

—*ALBERT EINSTEIN*

Bruce Brown, who's mentioned periodically throughout this book, has a cult following of fifty-year-old men and
women who used to be in his PE classes at Hyak Junior
High. That loyalty has spawned nearly five hundred thousand
Facebook followers.* Bruce shares wisdom on team building, leadership, and shared commitment to core covenants.
Retired from teaching and coaching, he now consults for the
likes of the Philadelphia Eagles, NCAA champion softball
and baseball programs, and businesses around the country.
Coach Brown teaches, "If a mistake is made with careless-
ness, then take corrective action. But if someone makes a
mistake with full effort and attention, find a way to dignify
the mistake. The bigger the mistake, the more important it
is to dignify it."†

During summer 2002, Doug interned for the Seattle Super-
sonics in the basketball operations office.‡ There were only
four or five of them there on a daily basis: the general manager; the head coach; a receptionist; and Doug's boss, Rich

---

*The Proactive Coaching Facebook page is full of wisdom for coaches,
athletes, parents, and leaders. The number of followers when we wrote
this book was 509,513.
†Bruce also implores us to "never embarrass a willing learner."
‡Seattle once had an NBA franchise.

Cho (the assistant GM). The team president, Wally Walker, had brought Doug in because "the price was right" (he worked for free that summer and might not have given them their money's worth). Rich didn't always know what to do with him. One time Doug spent several days scraping names of guys who had retired or left the league off of small placards. Then he glued on new letters (incoming rookies) for the upcoming NBA draft. It wasn't lost on Doug that the Sonics were paying benchwarmers millions, and he was contracting carpal-tunnel syndrome recycling $1 pieces of plastic. In 2002, the Sonics were six years removed from an NBA championship appearance and five years shy of drafting future Hall of Famer Kevin Durant. Not only did Doug work for free as a thirty-year-old MBA candidate; he worked for free for a bad team.

To try to make his mark, Doug went into Cho's office and suggested a potential trade. Think about how ridiculous this is for a second. He was an *intern*. The most important thing he'd done that summer was consolidating the team's salary cap spreadsheets from thirty different files into a single Excel file with thirty sheets. So Doug approached Cho with a thought: the Sonics' franchise player for the last decade had been Gary Payton, but Payton was in his early thirties, and the Sonics were going nowhere. Doug had found some guys on the Cleveland Cavaliers whose contracts would be expiring soon and recommended to Rich that "we" send Payton to Cleveland for an injured Lamond Murray, Michael Doleac, and Brian Skinner or Ricky Davis.* Cho looked up

---

*Expiring contracts meant the Sonics could drop them after one year and free up money to sign future free agents.

from his desk, grimaced, and said, "Who?" Then—in a kind way—he started laughing.

Doug's Payton-to-Cleveland idea might have been the worst trade proposal anyone had ever floated to a real assistant GM in the history of the National Basketball Association. We can hardly believe he said it out loud. And that's exactly the point. Rich Cho laughed, but in such a way that Doug had to smile along. He later came out of his office, tapped Doug on the arm, and told him that he liked the attempt. "Keep thinking about it."

Later that season, the Sonics sent Payton to Milwaukee for a young Ray Allen. It was Cho's idea and a genius move. He knew his stuff. Doug only worked for Rich Cho for a few months but felt he could speak freely to him. He inspired Doug to continue his quest for valuable ideas.

The Greek word for Cho's graceful response is *makrothumia*.* *Makros* means "long" and *thymus* means "indignation" or "anger." The literal English translation of *makrothumia* is "lengthened anger." A more interpretive understanding of the word suggests "patient tolerance of incompetence." As leaders, we build trust when we have a right to show anger or point out the inanity of a statement or idea, but we choose not to. Based on how bad Doug's trade proposal was, Rich Cho easily could have mocked him. *"Don't come in here and waste my time with your goofy ideas. You're an intern."* He didn't. Instead, he chose to dignify an idiotic

---

*We explored multiple websites to settle on an accurate translation of this word. Most of them were oriented toward biblical scholarship, helping pastors to prepare sermons. Thanks to Bruce Brown for introducing us to this word and its application to leadership.

trade recommendation from a guy who should have been across the office scrubbing plastic nameplates.* Cho's honoring of a nonsensical but honest try—his impressive display of *makrothumia*—cultivated psychological safety in its purest form. Trading away the team's best player for almost nothing in return would not have been wise. Cho was right to say, "Who?" and then let Doug down gently.

makrothumia:
patient tolerance of incompetence

But even more critical than letting people down gently is the fact that we have abundant opportunities to say "yes" to our people, and we pass them by without thinking.

---

*Rich Cho went on to become the first Asian-American GM in the history of American professional sports.

And every time you say "yes" or "no" to the people you lead, you make two decisions: a short-term decision about the idea and a long-term decision about organizational culture. Saying "yes" waters the roots of fearlessness. Saying "no," especially without explanation or words of development, gradually erodes the spark of excitement inside eager members of your team.

If it's not life or death, say "yes."

Life or death in your organization might be compliance, proper accounting procedures, safety, or numerous other nonnegotiables. So consider wisely when your teams speak up on the few most critical topics. But more often than not, we are dealing with other things (important issues, but not life or death). We could take on some risk for the sake of the bigger cultural implications, development of those we lead, and all the ensuing benefits of a culture of candor. But we still say "no"—almost reflexively. Laura Lothrop's boss did it when she said "no" to plant-potting instruction. 3M famously rejected the sticky-note concept for *thirteen years*. As parents, we say "no" to our kids all the time, often because it's just easier than saying "yes." In 2012, we surveyed hundreds of leaders whom we had worked with over the years. We asked them to answer the following:

> "At the times I hold back from speaking
> candidly to my leader, it's because . . ."

We expected the overwhelming winner to be "I am afraid of the consequences." That answer came in third. By a resounding margin, our respondents' first choice was:

"I do not believe it will do any good."*

That's sad commentary on the state of leadership today. Our people are shutting down because they believe that speaking up freely is a waste of their time. Don't let it be. Saying "yes" serves as a powerful antidote to the problem of fatigue that we described at the beginning of this book. Saying "yes" empowers, develops, builds engagement, and demonstrates trust.

But even when you just can't say yes (which should be rare), still dignify the try.

Over two harrowing weeks in October 1962, the Cold War turned frighteningly hot; the world came as close to nuclear war as it had ever been (and hopefully ever will be). In early fall, US suspicions heightened over perceived Russian nuclear activity in Cuba. But Nikita Khrushchev, the Soviet prime minister, assured President John F. Kennedy that the USSR would not even consider assembling and arming nuclear weapons on the island. Kennedy's advisors recommended healthy skepticism, yet Kennedy exited September with an admirable but naïve trust in his Soviet counterpart. Over the first few weeks of October, definitive photographic proof emerged: Khrushchev and Fidel Castro were conspiring to transport, assemble, and arm nuclear missiles just a few hundred miles off the coast of Florida.†

---

*The number two answer in our survey was, "I am not sure I am right." People are truly afraid of judgment and disapproval. When we dignify the smallest attempt, we prove it's safe.
†History suggests that Castro acquiesced more than conspired.

It's almost beyond a matter of opinion: the next two weeks were some of the finest the White House has ever seen. Kennedy led brilliantly through the Cuban Missile Crisis, averting armed conflict and guiding the world to a safety from nuclear disaster that has endured for more than half a century. Having learned from the debilitating unanimity that eventuated the Bay of Pigs debacle, the president demanded a menu of options and an array of dissenting voices. The team in the White House considered air strikes, air strikes preceded by warning, and several other options. They debated moral questions, strategic issues, and worst-case scenarios. Robert F. Kennedy—the president's younger brother and US attorney general at the time—described the gravity of the situation: "Each one of us was being asked to make a recommendation which would affect the future of all mankind, a recommendation which, if wrong and if accepted, could mean the destruction of the human race."[1]

As part of the deliberation process, the president stated explicitly that he wanted unfettered opinions. He dismissed rank and status and told the group to debate as equals. To make it safe—and to avoid weighing down the group with the anchor of his presidential opinion—he left the discussion for hours at a time. There were many voices from multiple angles. Ultimately, based on the recommendation of a majority of his team, President Kennedy ordered a naval blockade of Cuba and then massaged his way through frequent communication with Khrushchev and Andrei Gromyko (the less-than-forthright Soviet foreign minister). There were more critical choices over the following days, and multiple turning points, but the effective leadership endured. Kennedy navigated the dangerous waters adeptly, doing everything possible to provide the Soviets with an out and avoid war.

Adlai Stevenson, at the time US ambassador to the United Nations, came down from New York to participate in the missile crisis discussions. He strongly opposed an air strike or even a blockade, and suggested that "we make it clear to the Soviet Union that if it withdrew its missiles from Cuba, we would be willing to withdraw our missiles from Turkey and Italy and give up our naval base in Guantanamo Bay." Those in the room skewered Stevenson for the proposed course of action. It was the 1962 version of negotiating with terrorists. How could he possibly entertain such an idea?

He voiced the option because President Kennedy had *cultivated a culture of candor*—in its most absolute form. Stevenson's idea had immense value—it enabled the president to demonstrate that he truly wanted to hear every thought and every notion. The president dismissed the thought of a missile withdrawal and the surrender of Guantanamo Bay, but he dignified Stevenson's try. He shared with the team his own reservations about the value of Jupiter missiles in Turkey and Italy, and explained that he had previously asked the State Department to negotiate for their removal. But now was not the time—not under duress. In retrospect, it wasn't a good idea.* But in truth, brilliance, or apparent nonsense—dignify every try. That's the brand of leadership that gets people talking, and it rescued the world from the destruction of nuclear war.

_____

*And after all, if we'd given up Guantanamo, we'd never have heard Jack Nicholson bark, "You can't handle the truth!" in *A Few Good Men*.

What Rich Cho did with Doug's moronic NBA trade proposal, and President Kennedy did with Adlai Stevenson's suggestion to offer concessions, we must do with every idea: listen to it, consider it, and then—even if it makes us laugh or cringe inside—connect with the person who made it and celebrate the effort. Praise him or her in front of the team for being bold enough to speak at all. As Robert F. Kennedy explained later, "Although I disagreed strongly with Stevenson's recommendations, I thought he was courageous to make them." Again, every time you say "yes" or "no" ... every time you nod or shake your head ... every time you smile or scowl at the Adlai Stevensons on your team, you cultivate or weaken your culture of open communication. Even if an idea isn't the greatest, everyone else is watching. When you dignify the slightest try and make a big deal of every fearless word, you empower everyone in your midst—and inside some of them are brilliant ideas.

Howard Behar began working at Starbucks in 1989 and took over as company president when the coffee roaster was still an unknown independent. He spent many of his early days spot-checking operations across the company's expanding footprint. In June 1994, he traveled to Los Angeles to check on performance in the Southern California region and made a surprise stop in Santa Monica. On that day, every aspect of the store he visited impressed him, with one exception: he was curious why the store had a blender behind the counter. Earlier that spring, an assistant manager named Greg Rogers had asked his boss if he could buy the blender and bring it in. Rogers wanted to try mixing a cold coffee drink. He'd previously worked at a quirky place called Humphrey Yogart, and their cold-drink options had people lining the streets in July and August. At Starbucks in Santa Monica, traffic dwindled during these same months. Rogers's boss said "yes," and Rogers bought the blender.

When Howard Behar came strolling in and asked about the blender, Greg Rogers poured him a sample of one of the cold drinks. Behar's face lit up. He loved it. At the next team meeting, Behar floated the idea to Howard Schultz, the CEO of Starbucks and Behar's boss. Schultz said "no." He had two "important" reasons:

1. He didn't like blenders in the stores; they detracted from the coffee ambience.

2. Product development wasn't Behar's job. Starbucks was already working on some cold-drink options in conjunction with Coca-Cola.

Behar initially listened to Schultz, but then dismissed his decision in favor of listening to his employee. Behar was the second person to say "yes." He called down to the store manager in Santa Monica and told her to carry on with the drink in a clandestine manner. "Two things," he told her. "First, call me every single night and tell me the results. And second, don't tell anyone else about this."

A few months later, the Frappuccino accounted for 49 percent of sales in the Santa Monica store. Behar ordered a test of the concept in a few other markets and ultimately went back to Schultz. "I blew you off. Want to see the numbers?"[2] Four billion dollars per year later, Schultz has Behar to thank. And really, Starbucks should credit Greg Rogers's Speak Freely–minded store manager. She's the one who said "yes" when Rogers asked to buy a blender. She didn't say, "Huh?" She didn't say, "Just do your job." She didn't delay him and then forget to get back to him. She said "yes."

The Frappuccino success is a fun story. We had the privilege of hearing Howard Behar tell it in person when he visited one of our programs a few years back. He buried the punch line in subtlety and followed five minutes of suspense with authentic surprise. His reveal of Frappuccino and $4 billion per year in revenue create a buzz around the room. Starbucks dignified Rogers's idea with a $5,000 bonus check, a Rolex, and almost legendary status in the late 1990s. They made a big deal of it. In the colossal world of Starbucks, Rogers's idea had been a small hunch. But leaders who want to cultivate a culture of candor, which inspires ideas, must make a big deal of the smallest ideas and the tiniest tries. If you don't, people will give up before they ever get going.

BE GENUINELY CURIOUS

---

*We don't see the world as it
is; we see it as we are.*

—ANAÏS NIN

Remember back a few chapters ago when we explored the topic of judgment and disapproval? None of us are all that good at judging others (especially their intentions). Let's play a little game to reinforce the idea that our minds work in mysterious ways: please take out a piece of paper (or write in the margins of this book) and answer this question:

Is the tallest redwood tree more or less than 1,200 feet?

Next question:

What is the height of the tallest redwood?

Nobel Prize–winning economist Daniel Kahneman shares this experiment in his book *Thinking, Fast and Slow*. The question's content is immaterial. It could be Gandhi's age at his death, the depth of the Marianas Trench, or the length of the Nile River.* The peculiarity within the question involves the number reference: 1,200 feet in this case. When researchers asked groups of people if the height was more or less than 1,200 feet, their answers to the second question (the height of the tallest redwood) averaged 844 feet.

---

*Seventy-eight years old; 6.831 miles below sea level; 4,258 miles long.

Researchers asked separate groups this question:

Is the tallest redwood more or less than 180 feet?

This group's answers to the follow-on question averaged just 282 feet.

Social scientists attribute the 562-foot gap in responses to the *anchoring effect*. Given even a pinch of mental ambiguity, we subconsciously anchor our thoughts to the number at hand: 1,200 or 180 in the case of the redwood question. "Anchoring effects are everywhere," warns Kahneman. "The psychological mechanisms that produce anchoring make us far more suggestible than most of us would want to be."

In another experiment cited by Kahneman, judges even based their sentencing of a hypothetical shoplifter on literal chance. Experienced magistrates read a description of the thief and then rolled a pair of rigged dice. The dice could land only on three or nine. After each respective roll settled, a judge delivered a ruling. Those who rolled three sentenced the woman to an average of five months. Those who rolled nine sentenced her to an average of eight months.

Go back one more time to the murder mystery scenario from earlier in the book. We learned that powerful leaders talk too much. They suffocate the voices of group members and hamper team performance. People don't even fold shirts as efficiently when dominating leaders get in the way.[1] Your power is dynamite; it's a destructive force with a short fuse. When you begin discussions by announcing your own ideas, everyone else shuts up. You have subtly communicated a lack of curiosity about what anyone else might offer up. The team anchors on your suggestion and moves only slightly left or right. Leaders do this all the time, albeit unwittingly. Tomorrow, try it out on purpose—just for fun. Sit down with your team and recommend an off-the-wall or nonsensical idea. Sell it with enthusiasm, and then ask for input. It might go . . .

> "I'm thinking we should eliminate cheeseburgers from the menu and go with a healthier option like steamed shellfish. What do you all think of that?"

Our prediction: a few direct reports will fix their eyes on their laptop screens, a couple more will nod their heads and murmur, and one brave soul—who is silently stewing, *This is an insane idea that's going to destroy us*—might ask a question: "How do you think that will impact our revenue, boss?"

When leaders go first with our ideas, we anchor the conversation, and others instantly become hesitant to wander far from what they think we want to hear.* In order to be genuinely curious, you must cast aside your weight and let those you lead launch the conversation. Otherwise, everyone else's response to the redwood questions (and all the important things your team needs to discuss) will stay within safe distance of your own answers and opinions.

Instead of throwing out your personal pet notions to kick off discussions, leaders who want their people to speak freely should ask authentic questions. Authentic questions engender genuine curiosity. *An authentic question is one where you don't have an answer in mind.* You honestly don't know,

---

*There is a huge difference between leaders speaking first with vulnerabilities and offering their ideas: terrific for the first one, not wise for the latter.

so you're genuinely soliciting ideas and input. You're genuinely curious.* A spearfishing question, on the contrary, goes after a specific answer, stymieing those you are supposed to be engaging. Spearfishing demonstrates faux interest. It's also self-centered.

There's a story in Brad Stone's book, *The Everything Store*, that explains the author's choice of title. Jeff Bezos—CEO and founder of Amazon—wanted the people around him to execute a grand initiative. Couching it in almost moral terms, Bezos demanded that Amazon stock one of *everything*—literally every sellable item on planet Earth.[2]

With apologies to Bezos, the internal "debate" at Amazon regarding this idea is illuminating. People dodged the assignment; they hoped Bezos's fascination would drift away silently; they figured maybe he'd forget over time. The suggestions undoubtedly approached the comical.

"How about *almost* everything?"

"Anyone know where we can get some reindeer antlers for dogs?"

"You think he'll notice if we can't find a chocolate Kazoobie Kazoo?"

From a guy as powerful as Jeff Bezos, a suggestion like this carried the weight of a multi-ton anchor. It took time,

---

*Kahneman recommends another method based on the principle of independent judgments. He suggests that team members arrive at meetings having already written a summary of their positions. "The standard practice of open discussions gives way too much weight to the opinions of those who speak early and assertively."

and the specter of more pressing issues, to move on from the idea. But it was painful. Bezos originally dubbed the initiative "the most critical project in Amazon's history."* (The following scenario is hypothetical.)

> JEFF: Okay everyone, what's the most important thing we need to do during the next two quarters?

> MIKE: Solidify our IT infrastructure?

> JEFF: Nope. (Gripping spear tightly.) Not at all. We're solid there. What do you think our customer might need?

> BETH: Oh! Better service. We could look at reallocating some of our top talent to customer service leadership positions?

> JEFF: No. (Agitated and cocking his arm.) That's not it. What do you think of our assortment?

> PRADEEP: eBay has an expansive offering. Maybe we should plan a strategic response to their third-party merchant system?

> JEFF: No. No. No. No! We need to go out and get one of every item on the planet! (Thrusting spear into target.)

Jeff Bezos's original question looks authentic, but it's not. He has an answer in mind, and he's simply trying to get

---

*You can read about "Project Fargo" on pages 81–82 of *The Everything Store: Jeff Bezos and the Amazon Age*. The well-written account contains a number of Speak Freely lessons.

someone to say it for him. It gets worse from there as the others try to figure out what he's searching for. Spearfishing questions render people timid and afraid to miss the mark. They are the kiss of death for a teacher in the classroom and a prescription for dry, uninspired conversation in discussions with those you lead. Instead, ask authentic questions:

"What led us to miss that number?"

"How can we do better?"

"What was your thought process behind
the timing of that launch?"

"What should be our operational focus
during the next two quarters?"

Authentic questions are a critical tool in your quest to inspire ideas and cultivate candor. Don't lead off with your own thoughts. Don't spearfish for the answers you want. Ask authentically, and tell your people to call you on it when it's obvious that you're spearfishing.

Doug coached a fourth-grade basketball team one year. Nine or ten is about the age you start teaching kids to think critically and make their own decisions on the court. During a scrimmage one evening, a young player named Cade passed up an open shot. Doug had been constantly encouraging the kids to shoot when they had a "good look at the basket," and Cade in particular tended to hold back. Doug almost corrected him: "Cade, take that shot!" But something stopped him. Instead, he asked, "Cade, why didn't you take that shot?" It was an authentic question.

Cade lowered his head a bit, looked up at Doug, and grumbled, "Coach, I lost my balance and thought I would miss it. So I passed."

Doug had come a brain twitch away from taking the easy route: telling Cade what to do. He would have confused him, frustrated him, and missed an opportunity to let him speak freely. He got lucky and learned a terrific lesson: authentic questions are an invaluable tool in the quest to cultivate candor.

As leaders, we shouldn't have to get lucky as Doug did with Cade. We must *really listen* to what our people say. Candid communication won't come in unmitigated form until you've built truly trusting relationships with those you lead. It will start with hints, and we must follow up on those signals with authentic inquiry.

We fully understand that leadership isn't all about asking questions, deferring, and listening. We'd be better off if leaders did more of those things, but ultimately leaders have to decide, direct, and execute. Leaders also are held accountable for the results. But when gathering ideas, innovating, and developing people and culture, habits like anchoring and spearfishing are completely detrimental. Be part of the teams you lead, but don't dominate them.

By the way, because we figure you're wondering, if you haven't already looked it up, the tallest redwood in the world has a name—Hyperion—and lives in Redwood National Park, California. It's somewhere around six hundred years old and at last measurement back in 2006 was 379.7 feet. But trees don't hit puberty until they turn seven hundred, so it's still got some growing to do.

Being genuinely curious is about *how*, and it's also about *who* might surprise you with his or her thoughts, ideas, and feedback.

Ralph and Cheryl Broetje's apple business packs more than forty thousand boxes of ripe fruit per day. They farm over six thousand acres, harvest a dozen apple varieties, and employ more than one thousand workers year-round and fifteen hundred more during harvest. With a good crop, the company brings in annual revenues surpassing $100 million. They started this all in 1968 with no farming experience and no money. But selling apples isn't all the Broetjes do. The orchard they built from scratch includes housing for two hundred families, a day care center, an elementary school, a convenience store, a community center, a chapel, and a post office. They've built entire neighborhoods in nearby cities to help revitalize downtrodden neighborhoods and offer opportunities for first-time home buyers who have difficulty qualifying for conventional bank loans. They've also set up housing for hundreds of refugees from all over the world.

The company's nonprofit—the Vista Hermosa Foundation —oversees charities and other efforts in the United States, Mexico, Kenya, Egypt, and the Philippines. Their three decades' worth of charitable contributions have surpassed $100 million. They've led major efforts to establish clean drinking water infrastructures in developing nations and built safe houses in poverty-stricken areas for young girls whose fate would otherwise likely include some form of sex trafficking.

Ralph and Cheryl have tended to dying people—literally —alongside Mother Teresa in Calcutta. Cheryl is a self-proclaimed "believer in dreams," and Ralph runs his apple company having never owned a cell phone or a computer. No joke. When they started—the same year the United States put a man on the moon—the Broetjes aspired to simply pay their bills. Within a few years they were doing that. A couple more years and they were out of debt and had a savings account. A year later they built a nice big house on a bluff overlooking a beautiful river.

In the early 1980s, farming demographics started to shift. Men from Central America began showing up at Broetje Orchards in search of a living wage and a better life. Their native communities south of the border lacked infrastructure. There were no roads to good markets. Many families had been kicked off their land. The water table was horribly inconsistent, and coercive powers and corrupt politicians littered their lives. In the United States, economic conditions had also shifted agricultural practices. Gas prices surged, and migrant farming families that once followed weather patterns across the nation stopped driving from farm to farm and state to state. By the time they paid for gas and dealt with the costs and stresses of constantly being on the go, the American families decided they were better off heading into cities, settling down, and finding alternative jobs. Almost without warning, farms now desperately needed workers— such as the immigrants from Central America—to support their growing businesses.

In a serendipitously smooth transition, a Latino version of the migrant families flooded into the orchards in place of the American one. Business continued to boom for the Broetjes, and the new workers drove the success. Soon after this demographic shift, the company started packing its own fruit, adding a plant that could handle high volumes of apples each day. This vertical integration created one hundred new jobs, but the farm already scraped and clawed to fill its picking positions. Sitting on the sidelines was a mostly untapped human resource: women. The Broetjes were soon putting both halves of married couples to work. And as the women became employees, Ralph and Cheryl Broetje started to gather new information. The women spoke more openly than the men, and the information went way beyond apples. The owners learned of ghastly living conditions, mental health situations, domestic violence, and alcoholism. They heard about families sleeping in garages where rats and other rodents bit young children throughout cold winter nights. They learned of older siblings being pulled out of school to babysit younger ones while the parents worked. They discovered that the high school dropout rate of their employees' children approached 80 percent.

With loads of painful new knowledge, the Broetjes swiftly enacted solutions. They borrowed. They invested. They borrowed some more. They built the on-site day care center, followed by the initial neighborhood of houses, then a preschool and a private elementary school. This aggressive project continued until they had completed an entire on-site community, outfitted with single-family homes, greenbelts, after-school programs, sports leagues, and evening potlucks. They capped it off with the Vista Hermosa Foundation—*vista hermosa* is Spanish for "a beautiful view"—named by the families in their community.

In 1987, inside an apple-packing plant near Prescott, Washington, an unexpected spark lit an inferno of unconventional wisdom and compassion that has burned fiercely for thirty years at Broetje Orchards. This spark forever changed the way Ralph and Cheryl ran their company. What began as an entrepreneurial journey to make a little cash has become perhaps the best servant-leadership story on the planet. "We hired mostly women to work in the packing plant," Cheryl explains, "and they began to talk. They spoke up and shared their stories with us. And we listened." It dignified the slightest try in monumental fashion. Imagine the psychological safety imprinted on people's hearts and minds when a leader's response to hearing about biting rats is to build two hundred homes.

The United States Army learned a similar lesson—about untapped pockets of ideas and input—while fighting the war on terror in Afghanistan. Gathering intelligence in the years following September 11, 2001, Army Special Forces units were underutilizing a full 50 percent of intelligence resources: the women in the villages and towns. Cultural prohibitions against interaction with men constituted an almost impenetrable barrier. Not only was the valuable information these women possessed going to waste, but the enemy effectively spread disinformation among these mothers, sisters, and wives. If the women decided the Americans weren't to be trusted—and told their husbands as much—it could prove a major barrier in working with the Afghan men as well. So in 2011, General Stanley McChrystal launched Cultural Support Teams (CSTs)—small squads of the US Army's most elite women—serving alongside Special Forces operators.

The women were deployed into the depths of the war and built trusting friendships with the Afghan females who had completely avoided the military men. "CSTs have proven to be a remarkable effects multiplier everywhere they've been employed," observed an army spokesman a few years later. "They question women, help identify targets, calm tensions, and protect children."

Somewhere amid the people you lead hides a wealth of untapped potential. As we learned earlier from Deb Gruenfeld: Whether an argument is persuasive is rarely a reflection of its quality; many arguments aren't even heard until the right person makes them. And who are the "right" people? They are those with status, which ends up being fool's gold, because the people who talk the most, talk first, or dress in the right clothes end up gaining influence in the eyes of leaders and team members.

Introverts and newcomers are the packing-plant workers and Afghan women of your world—the valuable minds being overlooked. We don't see introverts because they are quiet, and we miss newcomers because they don't yet know enough (or so we think).* The succinctness and brevity of introverts and the lack of credibility among newcomers also reduce these people's status—and we know what happens when those without status speak: absolutely nothing.

---

*We often bring in newcomers for their fresh perspectives but then quiet them until they've "learned the ropes." By that time, they're no longer new and their perspective is no longer fresh.

We tune them out. "Our thoughts are shackled by the familiar," observes Jonah Lehrer in his book *Imagine*.[3] Insights we referenced earlier in the book recommend that people disguise their new ideas as old ideas to overcome these shackles.*

Karim Lakhani of Harvard Business School zeroed in on the problem. "Everyone dislikes novelty," Lakhani explained to the *Atlantic*, "[but] experts tend to be over-critical of proposals in their own domain." Our egos get in the way. New ideas—and ideas from new people—suggest that perhaps our tried-and-true wasn't good enough. It's a classic cause of resistance to change. And for the purposes of this book, you're the expert, and your disdain for fresh ideas is likely killing the spirit of your newcomers. And it's a problem, because as Jonah Lehrer and the loads of research he uncovered attest, newcomers have some of the best ideas. They're just not the "right" people.

This is classic organizational behavior. We write off dismissal of these groups as normal and advise the newcomers and introverts to ally with a person of influence. We tell them to build a coalition with those of status and then pitch ideas or share thoughts, and then we even call this suggestion to play politics *mentorship*. Work the organization, we counsel, and say the right things in the right way when the time comes.†

---

*Lehrer's book was pulled from distribution channels when he admitted to fabricating quotes by Bob Dylan. He shouldn't have done that, but it's a really good book and is still available on Amazon.

†We admit to having no idea how often people successfully pull off these tactics versus how often ideas and suggestions die a sad death born of frustration turned to apathy.

Experienced leaders sometimes just fail to hear—their dismissal of new ideas isn't even semiconscious; it's buried deeper. Our familiarity creates a special sort of tone-deafness. Have you ever been on a drive in the car and one of your favorite songs comes on—a classic.* You start to sing the first few words, and seemingly seconds later the song is over—you missed it entirely (even if you sang along the whole time). This happens to experienced leaders in the realm of new-idea discussion. If we've been around long enough, we listen to people but don't really hear them. Inspire the newcomers and introverts to dive in, and you'll hear a whole new song.

We're nearing the end of this book. If you've made it this far, we hope you're writing in the margins, reflecting, and growing as a leader. As you count down the pages, we will make this last point plainly: to draw out your introverts and your newcomers (and those hiding for other reasons we've already covered), you need to do something simple—you need to *care*. Don't let them hide, and don't dismiss them because they're not the high-status members of your team. Go get them.

---

*For Doug it's Guns N' Roses' "Sweet Child O' Mine." Matt prefers the sweet melody of Jack Johnson's "As I Was Saying."

THE PROMISED LAND

We delight in the beauty of the butterfly, but rarely admit the changes it has gone through to achieve that beauty.

—*MAYA ANGELOU*, RAINBOW IN THE CLOUD

Bruce Brown, the legendary coach and teacher
we've mentioned in this book, has built up a lifetime of wisdom cultivating cultures. He's coached hundreds of athletic teams ranging from football to basketball to baseball to volleyball. His former players have gone on to play at Harvard and in the NBA, and to coach in the NFL.* Like a lot of gym teachers, he's an unbeatable badminton player. One afternoon, about ten years into his education career, he was on his way to a volleyball practice with "bad day" written all over his face. It wasn't a sad sort of bad day; for some reason Coach Brown was just ticked off and annoyed. Janelle, a setter on the team—and by no means the best payer—ran by Brown and patted him on the shoulder. She could sense her coach's mood in the stiffness of his gait. His return greeting to her fell far short of his normal enthusiasm. So fourteen-year-old Janelle stopped on a dime, pirouetted, and looked her coach in the eye:

"What's wrong, coach?"

"I'm having a bad day," huffed Brown.

"How bad?" Janelle asked.

---

*Jim Mora, former coach of the Atlanta Falcons and Seattle Seahawks, and the current football coach at UCLA.

"Pretty bad."

"Well, you know what? I'm sorry about that. But we
need you for the next two hours. Get over it!"

And then she turned and kept running toward the gym.
Janelle was a ninth-grade youngster who believed so much
in what the team was doing that she refused to let her coach
slide. Through the organization he's built during the second
half of his life—Proactive Coaching—Brown helps teams and
businesses develop what he calls "core covenants"—immutable
ways of going about their business. That year, the junior varsity
volleyball team had agreed upon enthusiasm as one of its own
covenants. When lived out, it meant that every member of the
squad would be engaged from the first minute of practice until
the last. If players (or the coach) weren't "feeling it," they were
to "flip the switch."

"Nobody's exempt from accountability on great teams,"
challenges Brown. "On that day, Janelle made sure she held
me accountable." You don't become weak when you cultivate
a culture of candor. Rather, you have to become incredibly
strong. Coach Brown faced the rightful but piercing admon-
ishment of his fourteen-year-old volleyball player and had
the humility and courage to listen and adjust course. That is
what an inspiring, Speak Freely culture behaves like.

Culture, however, is an important but often misused
word. The modern-day authority is Edgar Schein, formerly
of MIT.[1] He explains that true organizational culture lies in
the shared beliefs of group members—what he describes as
"basic underlying assumptions." "If a basic assumption comes
to be strongly held in a group, members will find behavior

based on any other premise inconceivable." Michael Watkins of Harvard argues for a similar understanding, likening culture to an organizational immune system: "It prevents 'wrong thinking' and the 'wrong people' from entering the organization in the first place."

When you've reached the Promised Land, your people understand that it's valued, expected, and safe to speak freely—about anything at all. Wrong thinking consists of hiding thoughts, and the wrong people are those who shut down others' voices. Several years back, we learned of an interesting cultural-diagnostic device: *organizational conversation killers*. What statements—if made among your team, in your office, or around your company—would turn heads and cast a spell of awkward silence across the group? It's an ironic test given the Speak Freely concept, but we're talking just a handful of phrases in any organization.

As an example, let's start with some levity. There's a scene early on in the Christmas classic movie *Rudolph, the Red-Nosed Reindeer*, where an angry elf-boss checks in on his toiling-but-joyful North Pole workers. The golden-locked Hermey's productivity (and attitude) lags behind that of the other elves, and the boss is not happy. The angry elf questions Hermey—"What's eatin' ya, boy?"—leading to a public proclamation of the unthinkable: "I just don't like to make toys."

Hermey's statement jolts Santa's workshop into a frenzy. The boss erupts, and the others whisper loudly, "Shame on you!" At the North Pole, the importance of toy making is a basic assumption. It's what's measured, controlled, and rewarded. The allocation of immense resources (time and material) goes to the production of Santa's loot. Almost nothing Hermey could have said would have revealed the culture more plainly than his declaration that he'd prefer another vocation (dentistry) over toy making. His behavior and thinking is shameful. Here are some other hypothetical organizational conversation killer examples:

"Can't the customer wait a couple of extra days?" (Amazon)

"I'm sick of people smiling all the time." (Disney)

"I don't really care that much about tradition."
(United States Marine Corps)

"Who cares what Sam Walton said?" (Walmart)

When your candid culture begins to flourish, you will know it by the words that shiver the spines of those you lead. They will have come to find behavior based on the following premises inconceivable:

"Be careful what you say. The boss doesn't
want to hear stuff like that."

"Learn the ropes and form some alliances
before you start speaking up."

"Whatever you do, don't admit that you don't know."

"Just do your job."

To foster change within a culture, Edgar Schein recommends a series of embedding mechanisms. Schein explains that culture can be cultivated by things such as how rewards and status are allocated, what leaders pay attention to and measure, putting organizational systems and procedures in place, what and how formal statements are made, and the stories that are told (and live on) about important events and people. You can utilize these as ways to help cultivate candor and build a fearless—Speak Freely—culture.* But the *most important of all*—to this or any culture-building effort—is the process of *deliberate role modeling, teaching, and coaching.*

Which brings us to our final story . . .

Grainger, Inc., is a business-to-business distributor operating out of Lake Forest, Illinois. According to our research, its nearly twenty-four thousand team members sell roughly $10 billion worth of safety gloves, ladders, cutting tools, motors, janitorial supplies, and all kinds of other products each year. It's a wildly successful enterprise with a decades-long track record of rising stock dividends.

Like many corporations, Grainger enlists an external consultant to conduct annual employee-engagement surveys. The particular firm that Grainger hires services hundreds of other organizations worldwide. The global best benchmark for overall team member engagement—which measures best-in-class companies—is 72 percent. Doe Kittay leads the customer service operation at Grainger. In 2014, her organization checked in at 81 percent engagement. She's guided her team to an employee satisfaction rate that is nine percentage points higher than the best-in-class benchmark.†

This unparalleled success started out, to some extent, on the first floor of Building B in Grainger's headquarters

---

*Or any culture, for that matter.
†Given this particular consulting firm's measurement scale.

complex. "I can't really recall any other meeting I've had in the last three years," chuckled Kittay, "but I remember that one."

She has a flashbulb memory, in fact. She can recall what time it was, what she was wearing, where she was sitting, and the ache she felt after receiving the blow. "It felt like a brick in the head, honestly." One of her peers, who would soon become a direct report, had asked to speak with her. "I want you to know," Brian divulged, "I don't think you value my opinion. I don't even think you like me."

A really smart British colleague of ours developed an insightful model describing how humans respond to feedback. Mark Norton—a former Royal Marine and current HR executive—contends that our instinctive response to another's critique is almost always "Ouch." No matter how valid the input and how gentle the manner of delivery, we feel an "ouch." Sometimes the pain lasts for a few seconds and sometimes for a few decades. After we get over the "ouch"— or while it's still stinging—we move on to the "It's not my fault" state, blaming the messenger. In the end, hopefully we settle down and ask: "What can I learn from this?"*

Ouch!

It's not my fault.

What can I learn from this?

---

*We came up with the name "Norton Model" in tribute to Mark Norton, who shared this with Doug sometime in 2011.

Doe Kittay undoubtedly felt the "ouch." Brian's comment hurt. She drifted in her mind to some behaviors he needed to fix—and she eventually shared those—but when Kittay came to grips with what her future team member had said, she labeled it a game-changer.

> Brian altered the trajectory I was on. I thought I was good at this aspect of leadership—getting people engaged. I realized I was homogenous in my approach and wasn't reaching everyone. I had a responsibility to reach him in a different way. I'll never forget that as long as I live.

Kittay knew almost nothing about our book when we sat down to hear her story. We point this out because as she shared her experiences, we realized that her success encompassed everything in the preceding pages. She's recognized the suffocating impact of her own power, the fear of judgment and disapproval, and the fatigue of her workforce, and she works tirelessly to overcome these issues. She assumes positive intent, and when her people make an effort, she dignifies the slightest try. Then she sets loose genuine curiosity by asking authentic questions of *everyone* around her.

Most noticeably, Kittay proves it's safe. Almost every day, she transparently divulges her inner monologue. "There are some things you have to hold back, but I share just about everything else." In the middle of a complicated and stressful reorganization—one that took close to two years and threatened people's expertise, egos, and livelihood—Kittay communicated constantly. She admitted that she didn't know and volunteered her own fears. "I trust people with a lot of information, and that builds trust in return."

"The type of information that gets shared, and with whom, sends a powerful message within organizations," explains Sandra Robinson of the University of British Columbia. Confiding in employees with business details, financial results, and other important information not only earns trust; it serves to build trustworthiness.[2] So how do you build a team that trusts you and can be trusted? You trust them first. Sounds a lot like the key to creating positive intent. It's so simple that it's almost silly to cite the research. But few people lead this way—otherwise, Kittay's team member engagement score wouldn't be such an outlier.

A leader's journey to cultivate and maintain a culture of candor never really ends. Kittay was just six months into her role as vice president of customer service when Brian suggested that she didn't value his input. A couple of years later, Dave, the person she calls her "right and left hand," stepped into her office. His feedback was unfiltered. It was everything we've claimed leaders should cultivate. Dave told his boss that she needed to step up and make decisions. "You can be too inclusive," he warned, "and you need to rein people in and make the call."

"It was hard to listen to," admitted Kittay. "I'd asked everyone to let me know what I could do better as a leader . . . but it can still be tough to hear. Despite the sting, I thanked him immediately for having the courage to say it."

She went to sleep that night and woke up the next morning, processing what Dave had said. She made small adjustments to her leadership style, and then asked others how she was doing. "I'd call them in after meetings to see how it went in terms of me stepping up to quick decisions."

You may be thinking right now that this all sounds somewhat soft—the boss taking it on the chin and adjusting her style based on the input of her team. And granted, it's not the norm, but we know Delta Force operators (not soft), championship football coaches, and Fortune 100 CEOs who lead this way. It is soft on the outside and strong as steel on the inside. *Comfort born of isolation and naïveté feels powerful, but it's the ultimate form of weakness.*

Kittay is not a rock wall—and that's a great thing in so many ways. She shared her fallibilities. And here's the thing: her team's employee-engagement scores are nine percentage points higher than those of the next-best department or organization globally, and double and triple those of the worst ones. She is an incredible leader, as evidenced by data and the feelings and admiration of those she leads. Her organization thrived through change and continues to flourish. Kittay's life might be a bit more difficult when people say what they think, but she's a lot better because of it—and her team is prospering. Awareness and reflection are difficult. Kittay proves that it's safe to speak up, she attempts to dignify every try, and her curiosity brings forth fresh new voices.

Her mom worked in a high school cafeteria and her dad served as a security guard. "The number one leadership lesson I learned from my parents is the value of hard work." Kittay is a biracial baby boomer from Denver, Colorado. Her mother immigrated from Japan after World War II, and her father is of German-Irish descent. Her ethnicity nudged her into four years of involvement with Grainger's Asian Pacific Islander Business Resource Group. She learned more than she taught—learned about a culture whose part she looked but one she'd never really experienced growing up. "A lot of the people I encountered in the forum had difficulty expressing their opinions in meetings or to their leaders. They thought they'd work hard and get noticed." When that didn't happen as expected, some grew disenchanted.

Kittay spent time trying to help those Asian Pacific Islanders who couldn't quite muster a commute across the Pacific—teaching them how to sell their ideas and accomplishments to those above them. It was helpful in the moment. The individuals suffering the consequences of cultural difference undoubtedly needed the coaching. Kittay explained, "They are not 'look at me' people." But must we really recondition members of our organizations so they can live out their roles as solid contributors to the team?

This is exactly what we hope leaders will eradicate with a Speak Freely perspective. We can teach nurses to communicate positive intent, help people smooth over the rough edges of their words, and provide cultural instruction to an increasingly diverse workforce. Or, we can place the burden on the leader.

Don't make your people figure out how to say things the right way, at the right times, and in the right tone. We're not even suggesting that you make them say anything at all. Rather, we are passionately encouraging leaders to build a culture that is all about those you lead and not about you. Go get those who aren't yet contributing—for whatever reason—and bring them into the conversation in the ways that work for them. Not because they must, but because you and your organization need them. Don't do it through the force of your will, but through the power of your inspiration, authenticity, and curiosity.

Doe Kittay doesn't need to be reminded that everyone on her team has valuable things to say. She knows that when group members feel valued, the team achieves better results. So she genuinely values every voice and seeks each one out. "There are a lot of people who think they don't have anything to offer. If you want to build inclusion, you have to seek them out." Inclusion brings forth creative ideas, newcomer perspectives, and the wisdom of introverts.

> I ask a lot of questions of people who aren't sharing things, but I know they have things to contribute. I can see it in their facial expressions; they might be holding back. I don't do it in a negative way. I say stuff like, "I noticed you reacted to that; what's on your mind?"

We learned of Doe Kittay through Jennifer Porter, a top-tier executive coach. Porter conducted a unique version of a 360-degree review with Kittay's team. Kittay asked for her team to meet with Porter collectively and provide feedback in a team setting (minus Kittay). After Porter gathered all the input, they would break for an hour and then turn right around and have a candid discussion with Kittay in the room. It's a growing trend and a great idea.* But Kittay's direct reports were confused. They didn't understand

---

*A super way to prove it's safe.

the need: "We can tell her anything, anytime, any way. We don't need to do this."

That's the Promised Land.

Don't wait another day. Cultivate a culture of candid communication, and do it now. The work is hard and humbling, but the benefits are immeasurable.

Notes

INTRODUCTION

1. Liz Wiseman and Greg McKeown, *Multipliers: How the Best Leaders Make Everyone Smarter* (New York: HarperBusiness, 2010).
2. Bob Condotta, "Seahawks kicker Steven Hauschka says going for it right call," *Seattle Times*, January 23, 2014, http://seattletimes .com/html/seahawks/2022741216_seahawksnotebook24xml.html.
3 Terry Blount, "Pete Carroll voted most popular," ESPN, January 28, 2014, http://espn.go.com/nfl/ playoffs/2013/story/_/id/10363366/ pete-carroll-seattle- seahawks-voted-coach-most-players-play-espn- survey. Chart used with permission of ESPN.
4. Jim Collins, *Good to Great: Why Some Companies Make the Leap . . . and Others Don't* (New York: HarperBusiness, 2001).

CHAPTER 1: QUESTIONS AND UNCERTAINTIES

1. Dan Lovallo and Olivier Sibony, "The case for behavioral strategy," *McKinsey Quarterly*, March 2010.

CHAPTER 2: GREAT IDEAS AND TERRIBLE ONES

1. Derek Thompson, "Why Experts Reject Creativity," *Atlantic*, October 10, 2014, http://www.theatlantic.com/business/ archive/2014/10/why-new-ideas-fail/381275/.
2. Daniel H. Pink, *Drive: The Surprising Truth About What Motivates Us* (New York: Riverbed Books, 2011).
3. Elaine Camper, "The Honey Pot: A Lesson in Creativity and Diversity," April 2, 1993, http://www.insulators.info/articles/ppl .htm.

CHAPTER 3: FEEDBACK AND CONCERNS

1. Collins, *Good to Great*.

CHAPTER 4: LEADERS IMPEDE COMMUNICATION

1. Leigh Plunkett Tost, Francesca Gino, Richard P. Larrick, "When Power Makes Others Speechless: The Negative Impact of Leader Power on Team Performance," *Academy of Management Journal* 56, no. 5 (2013): 1465–86. Tost et al. cite others' research on these points; we take their word for it.

CHAPTER 5: A LEADER'S POWER SUFFOCATES

1. The *USS Greenville*: National Transportation Safety Board Marine Accident Brief; Accident No. DCA-01-MM-022, May 2001, http://www.ntsb.gov/investigations/fulltext/mab0501.htm.
2. Adam Grant, *Give and Take: Why Helping Others Drives Our Success* (New York: Viking, 2014), 147.
3. David Maxfield, Joseph Grenny, Ramón Lavandero, and Linda Groah, *The Silent Treatment: Why Safety Tools and Checklists Aren't Enough to Save Lives*, VitalSmarts, 2010.
4. David Maxfield, Joseph Grenny, Ron McMillan, Kerry Patterson, and Al Switzler, *Silence Kills: The Seven Crucial Conversations for Healthcare*, VitalSmarts, 2005.

CHAPTER 6: PEOPLE FEAR JUDGMENT

1. Amy Edmondson, "Psychological Safety and Learning Behavior in Work Teams," *Administrative Science Quarterly* 44, no. 2 (1999): 350–83.
2. Malcolm Gladwell, *Outliers: The Story of Success* (New York: Back Bay Books, 2011, reprint ed.).
3. Daniel Kahneman, *Thinking, Fast and Slow* (New York: Farrar, Straus and Giroux, 2011), 79–81, 215.
4. "The halo effect," *Economist*, October 14, 2009, http://www.economist.com/node/14299211.
5. Craig Lambert, "The Psyche on Automatic," *Harvard Magazine*, November–December, 2010, http://harvardmagazine.com/2010/11/the-psyche-on-automatic. This article profiles Harvard professor Amy Cuddy.
6. Susan Cain, *Quiet: The Power of Introverts in a World That Can't Stop Talking* (New York: Broadway Books, 2013).

CHAPTER 8: ASSUME POSITIVE INTENT

1. Robert Rosenthal and Lenore Jacobson, *Pygmalion in the Classroom: Teacher Expectation and Pupils: Intellectual Development* (Bethel, CT: Crown House Publishing, 1992). The overview of the rat experiment and studies at the Oak Hill School came entirely from this book.
2. Dov Eden and Abraham B. Shani, "Pygmalion Goes to Boot Camp: Expectancy, Leadership, and Trainee performance," *Journal of Applied Psychology* 67, no. 2 (1982): 194–99.
3. Dov Eden, "Leadership and Expectations: Pygmalion Effects and Other Self-Fulfilling Prophecies in Organizations," *Leadership Quarterly* 3, no. 4 (1992): 271–305.

CHAPTER 9: PROVE IT'S SAFE

1. Edmondson, "Psychological Safety and Learning Behavior in Work Teams": 350–83.

CHAPTER 10: DIGNIFY EVERY TRY

1. Robert F. Kennedy, *Thirteen Days: A Memoir of the Cuban Missile Crisis* (W. W. Norton and Company, 1999, reprint ed.).
2. Behar tells this story in his book *It's Not About the Coffee: Lessons on Putting People First from a Life at Starbucks* (New York: Portfolio Hardcover, 2008).

CHAPTER 11: BE GENUINELY CURIOUS

1. See Adam Grant's entertaining and informative book *Give and Take: Why Helping Others Drives Our Success*.
2. Brad Stone, *The Everything Store: Jeff Bezos and the Age of Amazon* (New York: Little, Brown and Company, 2013), 81–82.
3. Jonah Lehrer, *Imagine: How Creativity Works* (New York: Houghton Mifflin Harcourt, 2012), 128.

CHAPTER 12: THE PROMISED LAND

1. Edgar H. Schein, *Organizational Culture and Leadership*, 4th ed. (San Francisco: Jossey-Bass, 2010), 28. Schein is a professor emeritus from MIT's Sloan School of Man-agement.

Notes

2. Sandra L. Robinson and Sabrina Deutsch-Salamon, "The Impact of Trust on Organizational Performance," Research Briefing, Human Resource Management Association (Canada), October 2011: 4.

Index

About the Authors

Doug Crandall is a graduate of West Point and the Stanford Graduate School of Business. He has led multiple units in the army and spent time in operations at Amazon. For five years, Doug taught leadership, advanced leadership, and Leading Organizations through Change at West Point, where he won the Excellence in Teaching Award and exceeded the academy average in every area of teaching feedback during each semester he taught. He's the coauthor of two other books: *Hope Unseen* and *Leadership Lessons from West* Point, which have sold more than fifty thousand copies worldwide. Doug has been published in the *International Journal of Servant Leadership* and written case studies for both Stanford's and Harvard's business schools.

© Lisa Monteagudo

Matt Kincaid holds an MBA and a PhD in leadership studies from Gonzaga University. He currently serves as an associate professor of business at Heritage University and has been a top-rated instructor for the past eight years. Matt's work on servant-leadership has been published in the *International Journal of Leadership*

Studies and the *International Journal of Servant-Leadership*. He also has led the efforts of four start-up companies and worked as a strategic-planning consultant for an array of Fortune 500 companies.

Doug and Matt deliver keynotes, workshops, and comprehensive leadership development programs via their consultancy, Blue Rudder. Their list of clients includes Stanford, Wharton, Columbia, Cornell, Duke, Michigan, GE, Walmart, McDonald's, Amazon, IBM, Riot Games, Lockheed Martin, Mission Support Alliance, the US Department of Energy, and many others—both in the United States and abroad. To connect with them, to learn more about their programs, or to download free Permission to Speak Freely content, please visit www.dougandmatt.com or www.blue-rudder.com.

Berrett–Koehler
Publishers

Berrett-Koehler is an independent publisher dedicated to an ambitious mission: *Connecting people and ideas to create a world that works for all.*

We believe that the solutions to the world's problems will come from all of us, working at all levels: in our organizations, in our society, and in our own lives. Our BK Business books help people make their organizations more humane, democratic, diverse, and effective (we don't think there's any contradiction there). Our BK Currents books offer pathways to creating a more just, equitable, and sustainable society. Our BK Life books help people create positive change in their lives and align their personal practices with their aspirations for a better world.

All of our books are designed to bring people seeking positive change together around the ideas that empower them to see and shape the world in a new way.

And we strive to practice what we preach. At the core of our approach is Stewardship, a deep sense of responsibility to administer the company for the benefit of all of our stakeholder groups including authors, customers, employees, investors, service providers, and the communities and environment around us. Everything we do is built around this and our other key values of quality, partnership, inclusion, and sustainability.

This is why we are both a B-Corporation and a California Benefit Corporation—a certification and a for-profit legal status that require us to adhere to the highest standards for corporate, social, and environmental performance.

We are grateful to our readers, authors, and other friends of the company who consider themselves to be part of the BK Community. We hope that you, too, will join us in our mission.

A BK Business Book

We hope you enjoy this BK Business book. BK Business books pioneer new leadership and management practices and socially responsible approaches to business. They are designed to provide you with groundbreaking and practical tools to transform your work and organizations while upholding the triple bottom line of people, planet, and profits. High-five!

To find out more, visit **www.bkconnection.com.**

Berrett–Koehler
Publishers

Connecting people and ideas
to create a world that works for all

Dear Reader,

Thank you for picking up this book and joining our worldwide community of Berrett-Koehler readers. We share ideas that bring positive change into people's lives, organizations, and society.

To welcome you, we'd like to offer you a free e-book. You can pick from among twelve of our bestselling books by entering the promotional code **BKP92E** here: http://www.bkconnection.com/welcome.

When you claim your free e-book, we'll also send you a copy of our e-newsletter, the *BK Communiqué*. Although you're free to unsubscribe, there are many benefits to sticking around. In every issue of our newsletter you'll find

- A free e-book
- Tips from famous authors
- Discounts on spotlight titles
- Hilarious insider publishing news
- A chance to win a prize for answering a riddle

Best of all, our readers tell us, "Your newsletter is the only one I actually read." So claim your gift today, and please stay in touch!

Sincerely,

Charlotte Ashlock
Steward of the BK Website

Questions? Comments? Contact me at bkcommunity@bkpub.com.

MIX
Paper from
responsible sources
FSC
www.fsc.org **FSC® C002589**

Certified

Corporation
bcorporation.net